THE
MEXICAN WITCH
LIFESTYLE

THE MEXICAN WITCH LIFESTYLE

BRUJERIA SPELLS, TAROT, and CRYSTAL MAGIC

VALERIA RUELAS

SIMON ELEMENT

New York   London   Toronto   Sydney   New Delhi

SIMON
ELEMENT

An Imprint of Simon & Schuster, Inc.
1230 Avenue of the Americas
New York, NY 10020

First Simon Element hardcover edition July 2022

SIMON ELEMENT is a trademark of Simon & Schuster, Inc.

For information about special discounts for bulk purchases,
please contact Simon & Schuster Special Sales at 1-866-506-1949
or business@simonandschuster.com.

The Simon & Schuster Speakers Bureau can bring authors to your
live event. For more information or to book an event, contact the
Simon & Schuster Speakers Bureau at 1-866-248-3049 or visit
our website at www.simonspeakers.com.

Interior design by Jennifer Chung

Manufactured in China

1   3   5   7   9   10   8   6   4   2

Library of Congress Cataloging-in-Publication Data has been applied for.

ISBN 978-1-9821-7814-7
ISBN 978-1-9821-7816-1 (ebook)

I dedicate this book to my brilliant editor, Veronica Alvarado,
who so lovingly worked on this book alongside me through many drafts!
Thank you for helping me find my authentic voice and allowing
this secret knowledge to be preserved forever in this book.

This book is also dedicated to my parents and sister; my personal
astrology teacher, Christopher Marmolejo; and my best friends, Chuck,
Rachael Burke and Gage Burke, and Julian Toscano.

CONTENTS

PART TWO:

THE PRACTICE OF BRUJERIA

—

INTRODUCTION

Welcome to my *brujeria* book! I am Valeria Ruelas, the Mexican Witch. I am a bruja and also a brujx.[1] Brujeria is the practice of natural, psychic, astral, and spiritual magic. Don't be afraid of trying anything in this book, as this is very safe. Things like candle spells, crystals, spell oils, nature, astrology, cosmology,[2] alchemy, and the tarot are all really beneficial!

I am very glad you have decided to join me on this quest—I can't wait to guide you through a spiritual awakening[3] and to introduce you to the *bruja lifestyle*. The bruja lifestyle is a way of living that involves doing magic every day, which will ultimately help you to be fulfilled and happy with yourself!

My brujeria is very easy to learn—it involves reading tarot cards often, casting magical spells from the comfort of home, using healing crystals, working with the universe, and overall leading a life centered around pleasure, joy, and learning. Brujeria is not inhibited by binary moral codes or religion. Moreover, brujeria rejects the notion of white-and-black or evil-and-good magic for a set of more open ancestral views. Generally the practitioner doesn't cater to a single religious institution or even to any gods or spirits in particular if they want total freedom from that!

Below are some useful terms to know to navigate the world of brujeria. When you begin this journey, it is important to learn these so that you can speak to brujas/brujos/brujx and buy supplies to cast spells even

---

1 Xs are used to make a term gender neutral and will be used frequently for inclusion purposes. The term *bruja/brujo/brujx* is what I will use throughout the book, to make sure everyone on the gender spectrum feels welcome here.

2 Cosmology is the study of the universe and its birth, evolution, and ultimate fate.

3 A time when you awaken your spiritual abilities and start to see the world in a different way, to the point where your entire life and vibration shifts.

if you don't speak Spanish. When it comes to the types of brujas/brujos/brujx that exist, this is only a breakdown of what I believe to be the most common, modern, and useful terms used today.

+ **AMARRE:** Any spell item that draws in love or keeps someone faithful.

+ **AMULETO:** An object made for protection or luck, such as colorful horseshoes.

+ **ANCESTRAL READERS AND ASTROLOGERS:** Astrology is a popular practice in Mexico. Many practitioners choose the label "astrologo/a/x" and incorporate astrology into tarot. Most study Western astrology, and some perform divination using ancestral practices, including with the *tonalamatl*, maize kernels, tobacco, the divinatory calendar, or with glyphs.

+ **BOTANICA:** A store typically owned by a person of color who speaks Spanish or another non-English language that sells brujeria supplies. Botanicas are typically found in neighborhoods with lots of Spanish-speaking people.

+ **CONJURO:** A type of spell or magical object made by pact with a spirit. This is also the name for the sets of magical words that are used in Náhuatl to work magic.

+ **HECHICERÍA:** A group of secret knowledge, practices, and techniques that are employed to dominate outcomes and people in a magical way. Both brujeria and *hechicería* have the same definition, but the definition for *brujeria* includes "actions realized by the means of supernatural power."

• **HECHIZO:** A spell done on someone.

• **LECTURA:** A reading; to say "tarot reading," you say *lectura de tarot*.

• **MERCADO:** A *mercado* is a large market space; usually it is exposed to the outdoors. A great example is El Mercado de Sonora, which is sort of like a mall of brujeria stores.

• **NAHUALLI:** While these may seem like things of legends, my research and personal experience have led me to believe that nahualli are real. *Nahualli* means one who has the power to transform into another being, usually an animal or an animal hybrid.

• **SORTILEGIO:** A direct translation of the word "sorcery." It refers specifically to spells and acts that modify destiny or make someone submit to your desires and will, including magical remedies. This word is largely out of use but is common in texts relating to Náhuatl-speaking cultures. *Sortilegio* also involves *adivinación* (divination).

• **TIENDA MISTICA:** Meaning "mystic store"; a popular term for stores that sell brujeria supplies.

• **TIENDAS DE PRODUCTOS NATURALES:** Natural or alternative medicine stores. You may have to ask for the brujeria items here since they may not be on display. Some of these stores don't carry brujeria supplies, but you can buy *yerbas* for tea and candles. I've included this here because these stores sell all the plants we will be working with.

- **TRABAJO:** A continuous amount of spell work to take care of a problem.

- **YERBERIA OR HIERBERIA:** This is another name for a store that sells brujeria supplies and specializes in plants in particular. *Yerberias/hierberias* are typically more common in Mexico, while botanicas are more common in the US.

It is also important to note that some levels of expertise in these areas can't be learned through books or classes. It is very important to seek out apprenticeships if you are interested in studying some of the more advanced forms of brujeria, and I will indicate in the text which ones you need to apprentice in to have a legitimate grasp of the practice. Usually this takes a few years, and in some cases, knowledge may only be passed down in certain bloodlines. If you feel drawn to these practices, you can use spells to draw in a proper mentor.

PARTERA/PARTERX WORK (MIDWIFERY)

This is one of the most arduous paths to take in brujeria. *Parterx* help people from conception onward, offering herbal remedies, *pláticas* (motivational talks), and physical checkups during the pregnancy and after for a few months of follow-up. The parterx assists, for example, with teaching the birthing parent to breastfeed correctly and supporting the new parents emotionally. Parterx are also ritual birthers, and they support the client in magical ways. The partera/parterx may perform the newborn's birthing ceremonies, such as burying the umbilical cord in a ritual or doing a traditional calendrical reading.

She/they may also provide natural gynecological care in the community. The parterx is usually knowledgeable in treating sexually transmitted infections and sexual ailments with herbs, *limpias* (energy fixes), and incantations. Typically, helping birth a baby is more than just physically assisting the parent. It also involves complex ancestral rituals to borrow the soul of the child from the gods and bring it into the body.

RITES OF PASSAGE PRACTITIONER/ LIFE SPECTRUM DOULA/COMADRE

This is a fun facet of brujeria. It also requires training but is a more social and emotional supportive role rather than a medical one. There is no formal word for this type of work, but most people who do this call themselves brujx or a *comadre*, which is an endearing term that means "friend." Those called to this work facilitate rites of passage, commonly for occasions of pregnancy, puberty, coming out, marriage, aging, abortion support, and death. Basically when these moments come around, the comadre works with the family or individual to plan a ceremony and then facilitates it for the person(s). Those who work a lot in the thresholds between life and death are called illness and end-of-life doulas, as well as abortion-support doulas and death doulas. A death doula usually starts working with a person when they have been given a terminal diagnosis and counsels, casts spells, and provides emotional and energetic support for the person until they die. They then sometimes carry out grief support work with the families of anybody who is dealing with loss. Doulas offer extended services, working with folks through all stages of grief. (The word *doula* comes from ancient Greek, but it is used widely in the English-speaking world.) This type of role can be self-appointed with caution, if you feel comfortable with your knowledge and natural abilities, but there are ample opportunities for apprenticeships in these areas, and I encourage you to seek them out if you feel called to it.

YERBERX

These specialists study botany and herbalism. If their area permits, they grow plants and make medicine from them as well as keep detailed records of remedies and their effectiveness. *Yerberx* are usually more trained in wilderness skills, as they find plants in the wild for their medicines. In many parts of Mexico, yerberx operate herbal pharmacies, and they provide consults to clients for their health and troubles. Both of my great-grandmothers were skilled in *yerberismo* and offered their services out of their homes, something very common in small Mexican towns. It's common for yerberx to keep an arsenal of yerbas at home as cures for fever, vomiting, stomach ailments, and troubled babies. Yerberx are usually well-rounded and can provide many helpful services like spells and readings. Some may specialize in natural healing methods like *sobadas* (medicinal touch applied to heal ailments) and egg cleansing. They may support and diagnose alongside a physician. This traditional way of healing things in Mexico involves a mix of modern medicine and faith in the herbal and magical cures.

VIDENTE

The term *vidente* or *clarividente* is used to describe anyone who has the gifts of prophecy and clairvoyance and typically describes tarot card readers, palm readers, and those who use their gifts with tools like playing cards, shells, bones, and corn kernels. The closest term to this in the English-speaking world is *psychic*. Someone who is a psychic has the ability to predict future occurrences accurately and also has the gift of seeing into different time lines. They typically know information about people without ever meeting them or can perceive it the first time they see them. This happens magically with an extra sense. They are even able to perceive energies and know things about people remotely. Psychics are able to perceive things past ordinary reality and often possess the ability to see into invisible realms of energy. They have visions and can experience other realities in which they can see energy and spirits. (We will dive very deep into this topic later. I just wanted to provide a definition for those of you who are very new to this.) In the professional world, the word *psychic* often gets used alongside *intuitive* as well. Psychics have been around for millennia in my homeland. The royal families often had a team of psychic advisors and astrological advisors who lived in the palace with them, and to this day, Mexico's presidents and celebrities have all visited the brujx psychics to ensure success.

MEDIUM

A medium is someone who communicates with, lives with, and venerates spirits—especially of the dead— as if they were in the same reality as us. These spirits are not something to be scared of, and it is safe to contact the dead for advice and to have them around you. Mediums open up paths for the energies of spirit guides to come into our physical world through their altar work and devotional rituals. Some mediums perform sessions for people to connect to their loved ones and spirit guides. Spirits are sometimes visible to others, and sometimes they look human-like, but they can also sometimes come through as strong forces of invisible yet undeniable power or shadows, and they may look and feel like energy only. While the practice varies, many mediums use an altar if they perform a formal reading for a client or group. The altar usually has a nice tablecloth, a vessel of water, and candles. To formally make contact, some mediums may use music, dance, plant medicine (such as a cigar or ceremoniously rolled tobacco or herbal beverages), automatic writing, breath work, spells, and meditation to be able to see and communicate with spirits. But some mediums can just "tap" in and connect without any aids. Brujas/brujos/brujx mediums often have altars fully dedicated to working with all their spirit guides; this ensures the spirits come back and that they can get payment in offerings. This allows the medium to petition their spirit guides on behalf of others.

Mediumship tends to be an inherited gift. It is possible to become a medium if you aren't born into it, but it requires dedication and mentorship from someone who can identify all your spirit guides and help you speak to the dead. I consider mediumship a very advanced skill as it is a bit overwhelming, and so it is best to proceed with developing this gift slowly after you learn how to identify different types of spirits, how to protect yourself from negative energies, and how to get rid of them if you have to.

CURANDERX

The curanderx is gifted often in *sobaderismo* (medicinal massage), soul retrieval, and spiritual advice. Curanderx are often split in terms of whether they embrace brujeria because most curanderismo utilize many Catholic elements. Curanderx would support people via treatments, *sobadas*, and even altar work to improve a person's situation, and they have faith in their spirit guides. Some curanderismo is practiced in groups. This is often a secretive practice that requires rigorous work; elders and leaders of the community get to decide who participates in this type of work. This type of practice is associated more with folk Catholicism.

✦

Before we dive into the actual practices, I want to emphasize that brujeria is an inclusive and accepting tradition. That being said, when beginning brujeria, please be mindful and respectful. I advise that you always do the following, to make sure that you do not culturally appropriate.

1. Don't use white sage unless it is gifted to you by an Indigenous person as medicine.

2. Don't wear headdresses (especially those with feathers) or use any culture as a costume.

3. Don't appropriate Black culture or language, especially when it comes to hair trends. Make an effort to learn about racism and colorism and how it affects Black and darker-skinned people.

4. Don't use dream catchers in brujeria.

5. Try not to profit from other culture(s).

6. Don't use spirits that are meant to be used only via initiation—especially those called the orisha—until you are under the guidance of a trusted source who can initiate you if you have been chosen.

7. Don't photograph altars unless they give you permission to do so.

8. Don't photograph private ceremonies and rituals.

9. Continue to learn true history and question history.

10. Make every effort to spend your money at Black, Indigenous, and People of Color (BIPOC)–owned stores

and prioritize shopping at BIPOC-owned botanicas and yerberias.

11. Attend community events and organized protests for BIPOC issues.

PART ONE

— THE

ESSENTIALS

OF

BRUJERIA

BOTANICAS, YERBERIAS, AND MERCADOS

Magical stores—called botanicas, yerberias,[4] and mercados—are often owned by people of color and are locales where one can receive good services and buy spell work supplies, books, and tarot decks. These stores sell yerbas (dried or fresh plants for spells) and candles, which are called *velas* (regular candles you can prepare for spells as needed) or *veladoras preparadas* (prepared candles). Here are some other items you may see for sale at these stores, along with safety tips:

- **AGUAS:** *Agua* means "water" in Spanish, and at magical stores, *aguas* are alcohol-based with scented oils. They are very beneficial to use in limpias and spells, and they function as sprays. *Agua de rosas* (rose water) can be found in most Mexican stores, and it is a universal cleansing tool! It is good to have this to cleanse your hands daily, especially when performing tarot readings. *Aguas* can also refresh an altar space.

- ***BAÑO AROMATICO*/BATH MIXTURES:** Proceed with caution and read and follow instructions carefully. I think bath mixtures are best made fresh and custom to your needs, so don't buy mass-produced ones and ask for directions when using. *Baños aromaticos* that come in very fragrant pouches are useful if you want to begin your spells with a relaxing bath to help you gather energy.

- **BOOKS:** Very safe to approach. New books are pure. Cleanse used books by leaving them in sunlight and bright moonlight for an entire twenty-four hours.

---

4 Sometimes spelled *hierberias*.

- **CATHOLIC FOLK ITEMS:** I'm mentioning these here because you will find them in these stores for people in more colonized practices of brujeria. Rosaries, prayer guides, prayer cards, saint candles and statues, and holy water are common.

- **CAULDRONS:** Always safe to approach. Cauldrons are great for brewing oils because they can take high heat; you can also get a cauldron to burn incense.

- **COLORED HONEY:** Never eat honey that you buy at a botanica, since the purpose of these premade honeys is for spell work only! It should be used for love and attraction spells and healing spells. Honey is safe to work with and can be dabbed on candles with your finger.

- **CRYSTALS:** They are incredibly safe, beneficial, and useful, and we will learn how to use them in many ways in the crystals section on page 35.

- **DOLLS:** Proceed with caution, as dolls tend to be more prone to be haunted objects. Spell dolls should be avoided by beginners.

- **INCENSE:** Super safe and encouraged! Incense makes you feel more magical, and it has a long-lasting effect on a room's energy. Incense should be incorporated into all your tarot readings, spells, and crystal magic.

- **INKS:** Very safe to buy.

- **INSTRUMENTS:** Very safe to buy, but make sure to use according to the "Sound Magic" section on page 10.

- **JOURNALS/ALMANACS/CALENDARS:** These are very useful and completely safe to buy.

- **MASKS:** These are usually made of clay, ceramic, obsidian, or glass, and are generally very safe to buy. Masks, especially those that are made of clay and carved in the likeness of the ancestors, can be very protective and can draw a lot of Mexico's energy to your altar if you don't live there. Be mindful not to buy masks that are from cultures outside of your own.

- **MEDICINAS:** In some brujeria stores, you can find *medicinas*, or natural medicines. Before using, make sure to proceed with caution under the guidance of a physician and yerberx or curanderx, and always check for expiration dates and cleanliness.

- **NECKLACES:** Proceed with caution, and be aware that some may be for African traditional religious use only. Always ask what necklaces are for.

- **OILS:** Be wary of where the oil has been made. It is not spiritually dangerous, but it is good to always ask if it is made from fresh, skin-safe ingredients and if it is made locally.

- **RITUAL DAGGERS:** Very safe to buy, but only buy them new. You can cleanse them in sunlight for two days, and this should take care of any previous energies. Use for cutting yerbas or for protection.

+ **SANTA MUERTE ITEMS AND CANDLES:** Safe to approach if you feel a sweet or enticing energy or she/they speaks to you telepathically. Santa Muerte is a loving and protective spirit. We will discuss her practice in depth on page 102, as she is one of the pillars of Mexican brujeria.

+ **SOAPS:** Be wary of where the soap has been made. It is not spiritually dangerous, but it is good to always ask if it is made from fresh, skin-safe ingredients and if it is made locally. I would be cautious if the soap seems to be mass-produced or doesn't produce a good smell, doesn't produce suds correctly, or is too cheap.

+ **SPRAYS/*COLONIAS*/*ESENCIAS*:** These are all brightly colored liquids. I suggest that you buy as many as you like and use them often. They are very versatile. I will be teaching you how to make some on page 73 under "Brujeria Sprays."

+ **STATUES AND IMAGES:** Proceed with caution, as statues can be powerful and draw you in for the wrong reasons. It is best to get several tarot readings before committing to a statue, candle, or other image of a spirit.

+ **TAROT DECKS:** These are safe to buy used or new. To cleanse a used tarot deck, blow on it three times hard and wish all previous energies to leave. If you like to feel the energies of someone else, like in a vintage deck, it is okay to not cleanse used decks. Follow your intuition.

+ **TAXIDERMY ITEMS:** Proceed with caution. I love buying rabbit feet for luck and rabbit furs for altar décor. The rabbit is associated with the energy of the moon. Animal bones or horns may also be available, but I don't use them personally and suggest caution if you would like to use them in your spell work or on your altar.

* **TEAS:** Buy with caution. Tea is 100 percent spiritually safe, but it is important to check for cleanliness, taste, and freshness since you will be consuming this internally. Also check with your doctor if you have health conditions, are on medications, or are on birth control to make sure the teas don't interfere.

* **WASHES:** Washes can be incorporated into your usual mopping routine on the full moon to cleanse your home, and they can be used on cloths to clean doorknobs to protect and cleanse doors. Don't use these in baths—use them solely for cleaning or empowering objects and spaces. For example, a "better business" wash would be great to use at your business if you want to make more money.

And now that you know where to purchase your magical items and how to use them safely, you can begin! Follow these easy steps to get started on your magical life! It is really critical that you start with protection and cleansing, so please don't skip these steps before doing anything else.

BUILD YOUR ALTAR

Your spell work altar is a sacred space where you will cast your spells and connect to the spiritual world. An altar space that is about three or four feet long is ideal so that you have enough room to place your spiritual tools for your spell casting. I personally think it's best to clean and change the altar very often! I tend to do this about once a week if I can, just to rearrange the energy and keep things fresh. It is vital that your altar stay clean. The best way to clean the altar is to first take everything off of it. Dust the surface, then use water combined with three squirts of agua florida and three squirts of Protection spray to freshen up the energy.

I suggest that you acquire the following for your altar:

- Tarot decks
- 1 large obsidian mirror
- Crystals
- 1 image of the sun
- 1 image of the triple moon
- Drums and rattles
- Colorful cloths to change up the vibe
- Firesafe surfaces to burn candles on
- 1 extra-large vase to fill with water (better if it's ornate and fancy for the feel of the altar)
- Spell journal

PREPARING YOUR ALTAR AND SPACE

You should write yourself an opening spell like the one below that you say every time you read the tarot or do a spell at your altar. Channel words that make you feel empowered and protected that come to you during meditation.

I begin by greeting and thanking the altar and the space, as they are the container that holds all our magical energy! Spray the Universe spray three times in the air and three times on you, and then start saying your altar spell. Here's mine:

Thank you, altar.

Thank you, room. Thank you, walls, thank you, crystals, for preserving all of the energy that I create in this space. I call upon the universe, I call upon my beloved departed, [I will say the names of ancestors that I know are my assistants here], especially my bruja/brujo/brujx ancestors to assist me.

Today I ask for magical assistance and I promise to repay you for all you grant me.

How to Do a Spell

Below is an outline to help you easily remember the steps for spells. You should set aside about two hours or longer for one spell, and it is ideal that your process is slow enough to fit this time frame. The time you use will be considered effort and will help you obtain what you want.

1. Decide the purpose and perform a tarot reading to inform yourself of how to do the ritual and the karmic outcomes of your spell.

2. Gather the ingredients and supplies.

3. Prepare your candles and other items (you can do this at your altar or a separate clean prep space).

4. Set up for the spell casting by using sprays, playing relaxing or ancestral music, and cleaning up the space so that it is very clear of dust and dirt.

5. Change anything on the altar that has to be altered until you feel the perfect look has been achieved.

6. Open up for your spell formally via a five-minute meditation or recitation of the magic words.

7. Cast the spell.

8. Concentrate on the burning candle, and make sure the candle doesn't burst (place the candle on a plate).

9. To finish, you don't have to do anything formal, just thank the universe, any planets, and the moon for helping you, and take a couple deep breaths.

10. Conceal your spell work from intrusion by saying this: "No enemy nor foe may ever trample near any spell I cast, nor spy on or remote view this altar. Cross the hands of whoever dares cast spells to block me." This is a method of psychic protection that is easy and will help you block the energy of those who wish to stop your spells.

11. Record everything in your spell journal.

How to Use Magic Words

Since most sets of magic words are short, I recommend that you repeat them as much as you feel called upon to do so. Repetition can help ingrain them in your mind and communicate to the universe what you want! Also change your voice and try out different tones as you enunciate so you can find the "voice of power" that will make the magic words stronger. It might be easier if you just think of the magic words as a slam poem: What gestures, tones, and emotions would you use? If you like singing, you can also try to sing the magic words.

SOUND MAGIC

Sound assists in concentration and in making the ambiance feel great for casting spells. Many people assume that meditation is hard. But as long as you don't make it overly complicated and use sound, it is actually enjoyable and easy. For the purposes of this book, my definition of meditation is that it is simply the act of sitting or lying down (without falling asleep) for a prolonged period of time and attempting to tune out your mind chatter and your normal reality, tuning into a more divine, relaxed, and insightful experience. I recommend you meditate in a semi-dark, quiet room in front of your altar with soothing sounds to make it easier to tune into your mind space.

Below are different types of sounds that can enhance meditation and the particular way that they work with the mind. Many scientific studies have shown the benefits of sound and music therapy: music and sound can heal depression and anxiety, aid in pain management, and even heal tumors![5]

In older times, music was played at most ceremonies and processions and at most special occasions. I also think it's very useful to play healing music and sounds in the background while you perform limpias on yourself or on anyone else. I will let you know below how each instrument can help you in certain types of healing or magical work. I also think it is useful to play any of these healing instruments in the background while you do other tasks. Make a habit of listening to them, because even when you aren't meditating or performing rituals, the sound works to cleanse you and your space, and to open your third eye.

---

5 "Healing with Sound, Frequency, and Vibration," Gaia, published March 21, 2020, https://www.gaia .com/article/healing-with-sound-frequency-and-vibration.

- **OCEAN WAVE SOUNDS AND RAIN STICKS:** Water sounds help calm the mind, and they are useful for mediation, especially before bed to help trigger good sleep. Water sounds help us recall past memories and dreams. Water sounds are also useful for soothing the mind after a bad experience.

- **FLUTE:** The flute is connected to frequencies of love, peace, and eternity. Furthermore, it connects us to those we miss in their eternal rest. It is a timeless sound and is therefore able to transport you into any time period in the past for visionary quests. A flute can also trigger feelings of sorrow. While it may seem counterintuitive to trigger sadness, it can be helpful for communicating with the dead and for meditating to connect to those who have passed on or for when you really feel like you need to cry to let something out.

- **SINGING BOWLS:** These are either made of brass or crystal. Singing bowls expand our visionary space and allow us to travel in the astral space. They help you connect to the universe and to outer space. They also have the capacity to heal and restore energy.

- **HARP:** The harp is not a traditional instrument in Mexico, but harps help heal pain. They are incredibly useful for studying and can help in memorization of material. The harp puts the mind and body into a romantic and loving state that is perfect for casting spells for love.

- **GONGS:** They are energizing and perfect for morning routines.

- **CHIMES:** Chimes are great for calming nervousness specifically, for slowing down the racing mind, and for helping those who have a lot of difficulties with entering meditative states or who have trouble receiving visions.

- **KALIMBA:** The kalimba helps with restlessness and anxiety. It also creates a feeling of safety, love, and closeness. The kalimba triggers psychedelic visions with symmetry, bright colors, and florals. It also produces activity during meditations, so it's your best aid if you want to have a more cinematic experience in your meditation with coherence and a story line (rather than a meditation where you just see different pictures).

- **GUITAR:** This is a very romantic instrument; thus it is useful for casting romantic and sensual spells. The guitar also increases your capacity to enjoy the present moment. The guitar speaks a universal language, so it is useful to help you attract friends and connect you to spirits and people whose language you don't speak. Guitars also help people express and uncover their emotional pain.

- **RATTLES:** Rattles are useful for loosening up dense energies. Rattles can also help you run fast and fly in the astral space. They also help build energy force fields to protect you. They are used during limpias to enhance the breaking down of negative energy. If you find a rattle for your altar and practice, you can use it to dissolve and send away energies. Focus on the areas of the head, neck, and shoulders to be most effective.

- **MESOAMERICAN DRUMS:** Drums are great for more exciting meditations and for when you feel particularly low energy. The drums were very important ceremonial instruments and are played during plant medicine ceremonies. They are warrior instruments, used to increase strength and stamina.

- **HANDPAN DRUM:** I find that the power of this drum is to help you see things with your eyes open! Thus it is very useful to just play a handpan in the background while you complete an everyday task like cleaning or reading so you can see visions and spirits with your eyes open. It is an upbeat and cheerful sound to meditate to. Meditate with a handpan when you need solutions to problems and to ask deep questions. The handpan elevates the vibration of other things so you can use it when a crystal feels dirty or heavy to make the energy less heavy and to clear spaces. The handpan is also connected to outer space and helps facilitate astral travel. The handpan increases creativity, liveliness, and joy.

PRE-RITUAL HERBAL NASAL STEAMS

The nose is such an important instrument of magic. When smells enter the nose they create wonderful changes and reactions in the brain that can benefit us in all ways! The nose is also a direct passageway into the third eye, so to help you open your third eye I recommend these nasal steams. Plus they really help cleanse you and can reduce anxiety. Doing these simple things before diving into spells and the spirit world is important.

You will need:

- 1 round large bowl
- 1 towel
- Yerbas

Boil some water and then place the water and all the yerbas in the bowl. Say the magic words over the herbs. Then place a towel over your head and breathe in the beautiful combination of herbs.

Please be careful and make sure the water doesn't burn your face!

VERSION 1

This blend helps you quiet the mind and relaxes you:

- ½ ounce yerba santa
- ½ ounce spearmint
- ½ ounce peppermint
- 4 pinches rosemary
- 2 pinches oregano
- 1 pinch valerian root

Incantation:

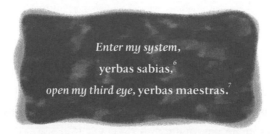

Enter my system,
yerbas sabias,[6]
open my third eye, yerbas maestras.[7]

---

6   Wise plants
7   Plant teachers

VERSION 2

This blend takes care of the third eye by stimulating it with cinnamon and centaury, which is the herb of centaurs, who were great astrologers, healers, and sages in Greek mythology.

* 1–2 cinnamon sticks
* 1 ounce linden flower (*flor de tila*)
* 1 ounce centaury (centaur herbs)
* Use the same magic words as version 1

YERBA READINGS WITH TEA

I recommend this tea leaf reading practice to open up your magical skills, help you read about your own life, and to listen to spirits' messages for you. The purpose of reading the tea leaves is to practice seeing things and interpreting symbols more freely, and to broaden your mind to see beyond what is literal. When done three times a week this ritual can really help you develop your visual intuition and ability to interpret symbols. Additionally, tea is nourishing for your body, and it is also very good at calming nerves, which can get in the way of spell work. Tea leaf readings can also be done for a client to answer questions or give a general reading.

You will need:

* 1 clear mug
* 1 star anise pod
* Tea*
* Finely crushed herbs**

*I recommend using a clear base tea, such as white tea, chamomile, mint, white willow bark, rose, lavender, damiana, jasmine, hibiscus, or green tea, so you can see herbal patterns in the mug when you do this. I prefer to measure out the herbs intuitively and by getting to know their taste and intensity. (Practice until you find the perfect flavors for yourself.) My favorite way to brew tea is to steep the yerbas in a teapot with a mesh strainer. Use boiling water because the bubbles in the water add to the magic of the yerba reading.

**I recommend any of the following. Start by using one and then using combinations. These yerbas all create beautiful shapes in clear tea: lavender, chamomile, damiana, jasmine, dandelion leaf, yerba santa, centaury, catnip, olive leaf, elder-flower, hops flower. As you practice, decide and note which yerbas are most effective for you and make these your go-to.

Rather than preparing one cup, make enough for three or four cups so you can read three or four different times, which is enough for a full reading. Sometimes the herbs can get a bit soggy so it's important to switch out cups when you feel you need to. When you do readings for yourself, don't drink the tea. When you read for someone else, have them take two small sips and then pass you the cup.

Place the star anise pod in the cup, pour the tea, then crush one type of yerba at a time into your tea. Let the mug sit for two minutes and then read the top of the cup by discerning what symbols the yerbas have formed. Draw them in a notebook. After making your first observation, give the tea a stir to allow the yerbas to move and form new shapes. Although this process seems simple, being dedicated to it will help you learn so much about yourself and about the world of symbols. You can always ask the cup a question and see what answers you get from the symbols, and you can double-check your tarot readings.

OBSIDIAN DAGGER PREPARATION

One of the items you absolutely need to begin your brujeria practice is a rough obsidian dagger. Obsidian daggers come in many varieties, and I want to encourage you to find a dagger that you really connect to.

This spell is for you to bond with the dagger and honor it as a magical tool. Perform it after midnight any weeknight Monday through Thursday.

You will need:

- ✦ 1 rough obsidian dagger
- ✦ Protection spray
- ✦ Protection oil
- ✦ 1 white candle
- ✦ 1 bottle dragon's blood ink
- ✦ 1 sheet spell work parchment paper or papyrus
- ✦ 1 small thin paintbrush
- ✦ 2 pinches stinging nettle
- ✦ 2 pinches rue

Spray the sprays on the dagger. Hold the dagger in between your hands at your heart with your eyes closed, and then picture a pale green light surrounding the dagger to transmute the bad energies. Meditate with the intention to give the dagger a name. Once you receive the name, write it down with dragon's blood ink on a piece of parchment or papyrus. Write your name next to the dagger's name and then connect the two by drawing a snakelike line between the last letter of each name. Then draw a circle around the two names. This helps the dagger bond to you and bring you healing energy. Spray the dagger, candle, and space with Protection spray, then add Protection oil and the crushed yerbas, stinging nettle, and rue to the candle. Charge the candle using these magic words in a warrior-yelling voice:

> *Before me lies my dagger.*
> *I bear it with all my warrior strength!*
> *All who threaten me may feel the impact of my dagger*
> *and face the power of all my spirit guides and protectors.*
> *I am protected, forevermore!*

Finish by lighting the candle and repeating these magic words upon the dagger once a day throughout the week until the candle burns out in a few days. Hold the dagger above the flame as you strengthen your dagger's power. Let it touch the fire briefly each day. The dagger should touch fire weekly to maintain its powers, so bring it out when you do candle spells.

When you're finished, conceal the parchment paper and dagger in a black satin cloth, and place it where no one can find it. Make sure to never lose your dagger's name and don't reveal the location or name to anyone. It should not be placed on your altar, but somewhere else more secretive, and it should not be exposed to daylight.

DOCUMENTING YOUR SPELLS

You can document all your magical activities with magical ink, which is called *tinta* in Spanish. The two most popular ones are green ink for money magic, and dragon's blood ink, which is good for all nonmoney spells. It is not made with any animal substance. For me, the best way to use magical ink is with a thin paintbrush that allows me to write almost in calligraphy style on parchment or papyrus (*papel pergamino*). You should record spells in both your spell journal (with a pen or typical writing instrument) and on papyrus/parchment. Having two records is great just in case you ever lose one! I also use my smartphone to document personal altars, spells, and readings in pictures. Readings should be recorded in your spell journal or in a separate readings journal.

LIMPIAS

Brujas/brujos/brujx serve the community by providing limpias, otherwise known as energy fixes, done through magical tools and their powers.

In Mexico, and in botanicas and yerberias in most places, the limpias are done in private spaces, usually at the back of a botanica. In more remote locations, such as Catemaco, Mexico, which is known for its brujeria and *chamanismo*, the limpias may be done in huts or outdoors; and often during solstices curanderx and brujx gather to provide public limpias.

I have used my limpias to treat colds, flu, pain, minor wounds, skin conditions, headaches, fungus, stress, menstrual problems, emotional trouble, heartbreak, and the effects of unfortunate spells. To see a difference in any of these conditions and other problems, the limpia must be done in the span of ten days, and there must be three limpias or more done per week for maximum effect until the problem is gone. Of course, for some things it will take longer, so don't give up fast. Start with three every ten days and then perform more if the problem doesn't seem to go away. I have had times when I only need to do one, so there are smaller problems which can be handled with less limpias and long-term commitment. I have also been in situations where I have had an unfortunate spell put on me, and it took me longer than two years of limpias and spells to get rid of it, but it went away because of persistence! Little by little I was able to shake the immediate effects of the spell; the unfortunate spell's remaining energy acted on me more subtly through the months. It is possible for a problem to be eliminated and then for it to come back, and this is not a sign of your inefficacy. It's just that some problems, especially if they are caused by unfortunate spells, can persist if the practitioner keeps casting on you, or if they are very powerful and can cast long-lasting spells.

CONSENT AND LIMPIAS

When performing a limpia, it is incredibly important that you create a comfortable environment for your client. Prior to beginning, you should let them know the details of what is going to happen so that nothing surprises them or is against their will. Please make sure to ask for consent to touch their body and to get close to them. If the client expresses discomfort about certain places on the body, you can stay away or heal them from a distance that is comfortable to them until they build comfort with you to get closer.

HOW TO PERFORM A LIMPIA

To perform limpias, always follow these steps to prep your space:

Set up an altar with a bright yellow satin cloth and a white sheet on the floor for the client to stand on. Fill up your giant glass of altar water. Spray Protection spray generously in the room, getting the corners up high (you can fan the spray up if you need, but make sure the room is thoroughly protected). Call all of your spirit guides into the room by using the rattle and your magic words to summon them. Set the ambiance by playing your favorite meditative sounds or songs while you perform the limpia. If you are performing the limpia on the client, have them prepare a candle with you at your altar upon arriving. Have a white glass candle prepared with Protection oil and rue. Write their name, birth date, and address on the glass with a Sharpie and light the candle before you start. Have the client hold onto the candle for the duration of the limpia. Advise the client to stay as still as possible with their eyes closed saying affirmations in their head during the limpia.

LONG-TERM LIMPIAS

Long-term limpias are ones you repeat until you feel a lasting effect. These limpias help with issues that are very difficult to face, such as frightening situations or traumas.

These limpias are most effective if you are also seeking professional mental health help. I advise you to look for the most welcoming care available and to support yourself with therapy, recommendations made for you by your mental health team, and your brujeria practice. Performing magic can make you feel purposeful and strong.

This particular limpia is used to clear unpleasant spiritual encounters and traumatic experiences. To remove deep-set trauma you can commit to doing this limpia once weekly until you feel improvement! The first time you do it, perform it thirteen days after the full moon, as the moon wanes. This is a good ritual to do prior to any spell casting to make sure you have clear energy. It is also a good practice after any traumatic experience or an unpleasant encounter. To remove deep-set trauma you can commit to doing this limpia once weekly for one month and see if there is improvement! Perform it thirteen days after the full moon, as the moon starts to wane.

You can perform this in front of your personal altar. You will be naked for this limpia.

You will need:

- 1 obsidian dagger
- Venus spray
- Solar spray
- Healing oil
- 1 bunch of fresh white daisies

Prepare an altar with a bright red satin cloth and an image of the sun or solar deity. Offer copal to the solar image, by either lighting incense or burning copal on charcoal. The image should be fed copal continuously. If you are alone and comfortable, remove all your clothing.

Next, spray yourself generously with Venus spray and Solar spray. Then use the dagger to scrape unwanted energies out of you. Be gentle on your skin as you scrape, and don't cause yourself pain. A light scrape where the dagger barely touches your skin works best. Work on your entire body starting with the front and back of the neck. Move down to the shoulders and out through the hands, directing the energy out a window or door. (Don't scrape the face.) Then scrape across and down the middle, stop at the pelvic region and scrape gently, then move to the feet. Finish by gently scraping your scalp and hair.

You are performing these scrapings because obsidian daggers remove attachments, including energies rooted deep in your subconscious that you have repressed or habits you don't think you can break; this is why we use the term "scrape," or the Spanish *raspar*.[8] The obsidian dagger also removes any lingering spirits that may have attached themselves to you, spirits that may haunt you in your dreams, or unpleasant things that can happen after trauma.

Once finished with the scraping, trim your white daisies, spray the daisies with the sprays (from about a half foot away), and charge them with the magic words that follow. Replace their water every day for one week or until they die and repeat the magic words to heal yourself.

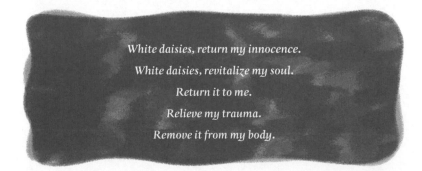

White daisies, return my innocence.
White daisies, revitalize my soul.
Return it to me.
Relieve my trauma.
Remove it from my body.

---

8 This word means "to scrape," but in a magical context, it is used to refer to when rough tools or yerbas scrape energy off of you.

> *Remove it from my bones, my skin, my home.*
> *Give me relief.*
> *Bring me into my body, to a place of love,*
> *clean me of all traumas that have shocked me and changed me!*

Dispose of the daisies somewhere far from your home when you are done. This is an important part of the ritual and should not be neglected because the more effort and care you put into this limpia, the better it will work.

Limpia to Clear Entity Attachments in Haunted Homes

This one will help remove attachments and entities attached to your possessions and your home. Say the magic words listed below, then do the same *raspada* but on objects in your home, such as the couches, the bed, even clothing and other areas that hold a lot of energy. In children's bedrooms, you can also perform raspadas on any stuffed animals or dolls, which tend to be associated with hauntings. This spell is to remove entities, karmic ties, stuck energies, and low-level spirits that have been directed toward you or anything that haunts your home.

> *White daisies and black dagger, send away*
> *all unwanted entities that have latched themselves onto me.*
> *Remove all soul ties that are not serving my spiritual growth!*
> *Remove all obstacles to happiness.*
> *Cut those ties! Cut those ties! Cut those ties!*
> *Cut them out of me, and lock them up tight so they*
> *may never harm me!*
> *By the power of fire, the power of sun,*

the power of my mighty ancestors,
I seal myself off to any unwanted and invasive energies!
I seal my home off to any evil spirits,
to any spirits who want to harm me or take things from me,
to any spirits who want to feed off me or defeat me.
I seal myself off! I seal myself off!
I seal myself off!
Forevermore!

✦

(Pause)

✦

White daisies and black dagger,
send away all unwanted entities that have
latched themselves onto me.
Remove all soul ties that are not serving my spiritual growth!
Remove all obstacles to happiness.
Cut those ties! Cut those ties! Cut those ties!
I seal myself off to any unwanted and invasive energies!
I seal my home off to any spirits with ill intention,
to any spirits who want to harm me or take things from me, to any
spirits who want to feed off me or defeat me. I seal myself off!
I seal myself off!

> *I seal myself off to all harm that has been wished upon me!*
> *Forevermore!*

After the raspada, spritz the flowers with Solar spray and Protection spray (from about a half foot away), and charge them with the above magic words as many times as you want until you feel the limpia is effective.

Replace their water every day and refresh the room with sprays for one week. Close the limpia by offering thanks in front of the altar.

As I've mentioned, dispose of the daisies somewhere far from your home when you are done. This is an important part of the ritual and should not be neglected because the more effort and care you put into this limpia, the better it will work.

Finish off your dagger limpias by anointing yourself with Healing oil. To properly anoint yourself, you should rub a thin layer of oil all over your body. Focus a lot on the important points, starting on the head: Dab the top of the head (crown), dab twice on the forehead—once above the third eye (which is located in the middle of your forehead between your eyebrows) and once on the third eye. Then move on and dab twice on each temple, twice on each cheekbone, twice on the throat, twice in the middle of the chest, twice on each shoulder, twice on each wrist, and once on each foot. Protection from these limpias is long lasting, but you should repeat them regularly, at least monthly. Afterward light a prepared protection candle (recipe on page 28).

ADDITIONAL LIMPIAS

Limpia de Huevo

This is the most common type of limpia and probably the most widely practiced in Mexico. In my opinion this type of limpia is most useful for helping with mild illnesses and discomforts, and for healing bad luck or emotional ailments.

Every bruja/brujo/brujx should know how to do this for themselves and for clients. Using an egg to cleanse the energy is simple so don't try to look for a deep reason as to why it works. It just does. The egg absorbs bad energies and then it is cracked into a glass of water to neutralize all of the energy before being thrown away. White eggs are best for this.

Pull an egg from the fridge and place the egg on your altar so that it can reach room temperature. Spray the egg with Protection spray. After two to three hours of letting the egg rest, you can do the actual limpia on yourself or your client. Hold the egg gently between your hands and connect your energy to it. Use these magic words to charge the egg. (Do this prior to seeing the client.) Say the below approximately eighty times.

I heal my ailments!
Nothing can harm me, nor take anything precious of mine,
forevermore!

Have the client sit or stand on top of the white sheet on the floor. Start by rubbing the egg on the facial features. Trace outlines around the eyes, cheeks, and mouth. Use a very light touch here. Rub the egg on your scalp and hair and concentrate there for eight minutes. For the scalp and hair you can use more of a scrubbing technique in little circles, not too soft and not too harsh! Then you will do this same scrubbing technique with the egg on the upper chest and make sure to focus extra energy on the breasts individually. The breasts are super powerful but can hold a lot of pain for those who have them. Then do the shoulders and go down the spine.

After about five minutes on the spine, move to the stomach, especially around the belly button, then the legs and feet. Finish by rubbing the egg on each hand, focusing on the palms. If you are doing it on the client, have them hold their hands palms up. Next, you will do an eight-to ten-minute rubbing session on the affected area (for example, if you have issues with your breathing, focus on your throat and lungs, or if you have a cut on your foot, focus there). Set the egg down on the altar. Say this when you finish:

I heal you with my care and my love.
Yo te sano con mi cariño y mi amor.

Lastly, crack the egg in a tall clear glass of water in front of the altar. Water neutralizes the energy of what you have removed. Dispose of the egg outside anywhere there is dirt, at least twenty feet away from the home. Make sure to throw three piles of dirt on top (so don't use the back or front yard). This way the matter is destroyed and away from the home and person. Instruct the client to burn their candle at home at their bedroom altar.

AFTER-LIMPIA PROTECTION CANDLES

Below I provide a standard incantation for various different protection candles. These should follow every single limpia. To strengthen your candle work, copy down the incantation with dragon's blood ink and a paintbrush on parchment and save these all in a sacred journal. There are many things that we brujx must protect ourselves from, such as a spiritual attack from an enemy, a haunting, or awful visions. These candles and spells will help prevent those things from harming you. Strengthen this by using your rattle to scare away any evil spirits or remaining energy and then make sure to shower right after performing any limpia on a client and use spell work sprays to refresh your aura.

Protection from spiritual attacks while you sleep

Cast on the full moon, at any hour after 8 p.m.

- I silver human-shaped wax candle
- Herbs: St. John's wort, hibiscus, boneset, wormwood, plantain leaf
- I black wax stick
- I wax seal stamper
- Protection oil
- Mars spray

Magic words:

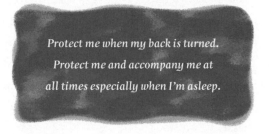

Protect me when my back is turned.
Protect me and accompany me at
all times especially when I'm asleep.

Make a hole about a third of an inch deep on the bottom of the human-shaped candle. Say the magic words to the yerbas, and then stuff them in the hole you made. You should use a pinch of each yerba, crushed. Use the wax stick to create a seal on the hole, so that when you burn the candle none of the yerbas come out. Just light the wax stick, drip enough wax on the hole, and then use the wax seal to close it. Burn the candle at your bedside table.

How to Charge an Object to Give It Purpose

Charging objects (such as yerbas) is useful in spell work as it multiplies and magnifies their energy. There are a few ways to charge an object, meaning to give it a purpose and turn it from something seemingly ordinary into a useful tool for spell work. My favorite method is by using just my hands, a bit of oil that corresponds to my purpose, and a crystal magic wand or a crystal pendulum. Remember your hands emit energy. They are powerful tools, which is why palm readers believe that the hand can tell you so much about a person.

To charge an object with your hands, rub two to three drops of oil on your hands or draw a symbol of your choice with your finger on your hands. Use the oil that best supports your goal. You then want to hold the object in your hands and concentrate on connecting to the object visually by looking at it with intent. Thank the object for working for you. Then say a meaningful set of magic words. (These can be any that I have provided for you or ones you make up.) Repeat it several times until you feel the object has absorbed your energy and is now ready to use.

A crystal wand or pendulum rubbed with oil can also be used to charge an object. Any of these kinds of items has a special power to create energy to be put into objects. With the crystal wand, you can repeat trace symbols or simply swirl the wand around in a circular motion above the object you are charging, or use it to direct energy into the object. Focus intently and repeat the incantations aloud while you wave the wand.

To use the pendulum, tell it your purpose, and then swing it back and forth over the object you are charging while repeating the magic words. Do this for at least five minutes.

WORKING WITH NATURE

Working with nature is really essential in brujeria. Although most of your spell work will be done at home, it is really useful to find a couple of outdoor spaces where you can perform your magic as well and to find places where you can gather spell work ingredients in the wild! For example, when you have heavy energy and you need to perform a limpia to ease it, it is useful to do it outside so you don't release energy in your home. Nature is also home to the most natural source of healing and cleansing energy—water. It is useful to collect water from the ocean, rain, and rivers for your magic. Every time you gather water, speak to it, give it thanks, and then take it home with you. Natural waters can be used to clean things both physically and energetically. You can also use it to wipe down surfaces like your altar, tools, and crystals.

Ocean water is a very romantic type of water and it also contains a great healing energy. As such, it has a couple of different uses and especially makes a great ingredient in love spells to attract physically strong, healthy, and fertile partners. It can also be used to entice back old lovers.

OCEAN WATER SPELL

This spell is used to draw in love or win back an old lover.

You will need:

- 1 large bottle of ocean water
- 1 large decorative glass bottle
- 1 red ribbon, about 1 foot long

Collect ocean water during the daytime and then place the water in a decorative bottle. Enchant the bottle with the following incantation:

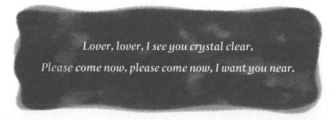

Lover, lover, I see you crystal clear,
Please come now, please come now, I want you near.

Then hold the bottle in your hands and repeat these magic words as many times as you can for fifteen minutes to program this affirmation into your subconscious so it can come to life. After, place your bottle on a windowsill. You can leave it there for as long as you want, and you can refresh it and repeat this ritual whenever you feel called to strengthen this work. Bring the bottle, which will build up energy over time, to your altar when you want to light candles for love spells.

When you feel its strength, repeat the following magic words for another fifteen minutes, this time using the red ribbon, which represents the bond you hope to attract:

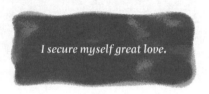

I secure myself great love.

Before reciting this, get yourself in a meditative state. Wrap the ribbon around your arm starting at your wrist. Every time the ribbon wraps around, repeat the magic words. Undo the ribbon and repeat, over and over again, until fifteen minutes have elapsed. Tie the red ribbon on the bottle when you finish and keep it for later use. I suggest love spells be cast on the full moon, but it is generally okay to do them at any time.

RAINWATER MONEY-DRAWING SPELL

Rainwater is useful for attracting wealth, business, and general luck.

You will need:

- ◆ Rainwater
- ◆ 1 small clear bowl
- ◆ 3 pennies
- ◆ Crystals of your choice
- ◆ Purple cloth

Gather rainwater in two large bottles to keep for later. Place the rainwater in a small clear bowl on your altar. Stack three pennies in the rainwater in the shape of a pyramid and any crystals that you feel will attract wealth. I suggest zebra jasper, Shiva lingam, carnelian, and citrine for this. Use this incantation to charm the water:

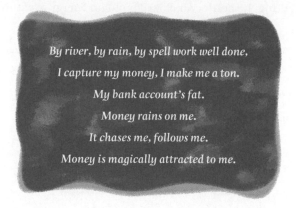

By river, by rain, by spell work well done,
I capture my money, I make me a ton.
My bank account's fat.
Money rains on me.
It chases me, follows me.
Money is magically attracted to me.

After you speak the incantation into the water, cover the bowl with a purple cloth. Every morning when you wake until the water evaporates, take the purple cloth off the water, and repeat the incantation to attract wealth. Refresh the water every two or three days so it doesn't get dirty. This bowl can be permanent on your altar since money is always important to have. This ritual can also be one that you perform in your place of business.

RIVER WATER PROTECTION RITUAL

River water is very useful for general protection and for breaking hexes. My favorite way to use it is to protect your home by rubbing it on doorknobs and doors with a red cloth. Each time the door is closed, evil spirits cannot enter if the door has been rubbed with river water.

You will need:

+ River water
+ Piece of red cloth

At around 7:30 p.m, using the red cloth, rub the river water on every doorknob and door in the house and say these magic words:

Seal the door.

Seal the door.

Trabajos, hechizos, and control spells be gone.

Trabajos done by other brujos/brujas/brujx be gone.

Greed, spiritual attacks, theft, and misery be gone.

Seal the door! Seal the door to unwanted spirits!

Hexes, jinxes, brujeria spells, curses, crossings, drains, evil eyes, and blockages be gone.

Hexes, jinxes, brujeria spells, curses, crossings, drains, evil eyes, and blockages be gone.

HOW TO RECITE MAGIC WORDS

Since most magic words are short, I recommend that you repeat them as much as you feel called upon to do so. Repetition can help ingrain them in your mind and communicate to the universe what you want! Also try to change your voice and try out different tones as you enunciate so you can find the "voice of power" that will make the incantation stronger. It might be easier if you just think of the incantation as a slam poem. What gestures, tones, and emotions would you use? If you like singing, you can also try to sing the incantation.

OBSIDIAN MIRROR TRAINING

An obsidian mirror will train you to see symbols and the unseen world, and if you are lucky, you can see yourself shape-shift in the mirror. It will basically open you up emotionally, spiritually, and mentally all while giving you healing guidance. This practice works best with a six-inch mirror or larger.

The obsidian mirror is very special because it is a portal to an alternative reality where we do not have limitations. Looking in an obsidian mirror helps us dissolve the "blockages" created by our rational minds, and it also helps with barriers of language. Additionally, it helps you work with your psyche. One could use the mirror to visit a loved one who has died in their reality. The mirror has a memory, so as you use it, it will hold on to experiences, remember what you say, and will make you feel more powerful and beautiful. You should also name this tool—the same way you named your dagger—because it will build a bond to you.

To start working with the mirror, spray yourself and the room with Receive Messages spray and Protection spray. Set the mirror down on your altar and sprinkle some dry marigold or calendula on and around the mirror. Let it sit for a few minutes. I like to look in the obsidian mirror both during the day and night and make note of the differences in what I feel and see. Daytime is slightly less frightening for those who still have a little bit of fear so start then. At night, looking in the mirror can make you see a lot of spirits, and the shape-shifting is very bold, thus it helps you see and feel the other realities and see your shadow/soul/invisible self. I would suggest doing the nasal steam that I discussed earlier before doing mirror gazing. The next part—working with the mirror—is very easy. I personally work in silence with the mirror. I don't talk to it or program it. I move my gaze if I need to, but I really try to concentrate on what starts to happen and what comes to me.

Do this gazing for ten to fifteen minutes straight if you can. A couple of minutes in I usually start to see animalistic characteristics; my face shifts and becomes less human. This practice is great for expanding your imagination and intuition, and feeling closer to your ancestors. The mirror can help you develop the ability to have visions. You can do this and definitely see more than with your eyes closed untrained. The mirror will become your health guide as well. One thing I've noticed is I tend to look at myself and really see whether I'm denying or suppressing those things shown to me so I can heal them. The mirror will always make you aware of things before they happen, so naturally it can help you gain an advantage in life and also prevent disasters, such as huge health issues. Conversely, when I'm doing really well, the mirror actually makes my skin look shiny and beautiful, which helps to show me when I have moved past something difficult or fixed a health problem. I remember one of the most profound moments I had with my mirror was when I started to see myself with blue skin. I loved it because of course that is something impossible in the human realm but possible in the mirror. This is why I really enjoy the mirror because in many ways, it is a direct connector to the spirit reality and is a really good way to start having visions. The other use of the mirror is its physical healing properties. I like to place it upon my stomach and then lie in bed and allow the good energy to move through me.

Additionally, the best way to heal yourself is in front of a clean obsidian mirror. Place it near your bedside, directed at you, and state your purpose before you go to bed: "Obsidian mirror, soak me in your healing rays." Let the energy of the obsidian soak you overnight. Do this until you notice a difference. The mirror can hold all of your rage as well and keep it from going into other spaces.

Whenever you're finished gazing into or working with the mirror, clean it with water, close your eyes, and close the portal of energy in the mirror; tell the mirror you are departing, cover it with white velvet, and then you're done! Never let others touch your mirror, and keep it on or near your altar.

Fixing Your Energy with Crystals

I can't stress enough how useful crystals are in the brujeria lifestyle. First, a bit of insight into their creation. When forming, crystals "branch and bristle as trillions of atoms connect in regular three-dimensional patterns. Each crystal starts small and grows as more atoms are added. Many grow from water rich in dissolved minerals, but they also grow from melted rock and even vapor. Under the influence of different temperatures and pressures, atoms combine in an amazing array of crystal shapes."[9] This is why we have such a great variety to choose from. I've created for you a master guide of crystals, starting on page 127, so you can reference this whenever you want to buy a new crystal or source them for your spells.

Using crystals is quite easy. There are many ways that you can use crystals to enhance your spells and to heal. Crystals assist in facilitating visionary states, and they also function as protection tools. Crystals draw in luck and work very nicely to heal our bodies (in conjunction with medical and mental health care if we need it). When you place crystals in the right places on the body, you can receive their benefits. Some crystals are sold "raw" so they retain their rough textures. Additionally there are polished varieties in the form of shapes or pocket-sized tumbled crystals. They aid us by simply being in our spaces, and using them formally in spells amps up their power even more!

USING CRYSTALS

As I mentioned, you can use crystals on your body to address certain energy problems. Each crystal will be placed on a certain part of the body to be activated. As a bruja, I hear a lot about people's problems, and so I have tried to design these crystal sets to address the most common energy problems people find hard to fix.

The fun part about performing crystal work on others or yourself is that you get to use your hands and pendulum to create and move energies around the person in question.

To begin, you will need a crystal pendulum so you can magnify the energy of each crystal. Spray a light pink sheet with Protection spray.

---

9 "Minerals and Crystals," Smithsonian Education, http://www.smithsonianeducation.org/educa tors/lesson_plans/minerals/minerals_crystals.html.

Have the person/your client lie down on the sheet, ideally on a massage table or a comfortable couch, although outdoors on soft grass works great too if it is not too busy.

Each swing or circle of a pendulum multiplies the energy. You should also use your hands to sweep and to move energy on the person as you work, for about thirty minutes total. To begin, it's helpful to draw circles in the air over the client, and then practice doing other shapes that help release and fix the energies and activate the crystals. Use your intuition for these movements.

As you go, join both hands at the thumb and the index finger and form a triangle; then, starting at the head, use this hand position to sweep energy down from the head to the toes and away and off the client! Direct that energy out a window or door.

SCRYING WITH CRYSTALS

I define *scrying* as "foretelling the future using a crystal ball or other reflective object or surface." It also includes the act of looking/gazing at a crystal or group of crystals, or adding them to a divination ritual to gain information and to stimulate your senses and visions. Crystals are capable of enhancing readings.

The best tools with which to scry are slabs, spheres, mirrors, and skulls. In order to scry, it is important to set up a sacred space on your altar to place the crystals on and to speak to the crystals as well as provide them with sound to amplify energies.

When you don't feel like traditional meditation, this is a more active meditation. Crystals hold valuable information, and they are connected to the world of the infinite, the past, present, and future, as well as to other realms of energy that we don't have access to. During a scrying ritual, you should lift up each crystal, hold it close, examine its details closely with your naked eye or with a magnifying glass, and allow your gaze to penetrate deep into it to see what effects each one has on you. Don't just gaze at your crystals from afar.

Ideally you will have visions and be able to travel through the astral world as well as hear messages that you need.

To start a scrying session, decide on your questions and intentions. Place all of the crystals in a semicircle, provide them with incense for seven minutes, vocalize your intention to them (crystals can hear you), and then sit patiently in front of the crystal gazing set. You can also play some music. Try not to complicate this, and let energy just flow to you. Even if you receive obscure visions or numbers, remember it all has a meaning that you can decode and that sometimes the meaning of visions will make itself clear later. Spray yourself generously with Receive Messages spray. It is helpful if you try to stare and receive with eyes open then closed for about fifteen minutes. You can spend some time closing your eyes to clarify things and to see more clearly what the guides want you to do.

TAROT AND CRYSTAL SCRYING RITUALS

These are some really useful combinations that will help you scry. Then you can pull tarot cards and consider it a full ritual!

Scrying Set 1
- Pyrite, obsidian, amber, fluorite
- This set helps specifically with communication to the homeland deities, messages about money and career, lottery numbers, health, and the future.

Scrying Set 2
- Smoky quartz, labradorite, amber obsidian
- This set helps receive messages about love. It also helps clear energy and identify energy issues.

Scrying Set 3
- Selenite slab, azurite, jade
- This set helps communicate with the higher self

and ask questions about one's past, present, future, and life path. Helps you communicate with nature. Helps you identify enemies and know how to take them down. You can ask the crystal to help you clear envy.

Scrying Set 4

- Gold sheen obsidian, sardonyx, kambaba jasper
- This set helps shed light on difficulties and family, relationship, and friend questions.

Scrying Set 5

- Lapis lazuli, orange calcite, white moonstone
- This scrying set helps you contact helpers for your healing work. It helps you get to the bottom of your problems and receive insight on how to solve them. It helps you improve your physical health and sharpen your spell work and spiritual powers.

Scrying Set 6

- Mango calcite, pistachio calcite, tourmalated quartz
- This set soothes the soul and spiritual energies and helps you to be brave and to communicate. Great for healing the heart and emotions.

PART TWO

THE
PRACTICE
OF
BRUJERIA

THE RIDER-WAITE-SMITH TAROT DECK

An essential skill to have as a bruja/brujo/brujx is to be able to provide tarot card readings for yourself and others. There are many decks out there, but my favorite to teach with is the Rider-Waite-Smith tarot deck. This deck is special to me because I see it as so much more than a future-telling tool; to me, it helps a person heal their past, present, and future, and it can lead to profound spiritual sessions[10] and dialogues with your cards.

Arthur Edward Waite was a scholar who wrote extensively on esoteric matters, while Pamela Colman Smith, who produced all of the images for the deck, was a visionary and psychic artist. Her work has spiritual properties and has been described as "the art of an androgynous sorceress, a prophetess who seeks and finds the cosmic."[11] It is the work of a true seer.

The method that I demonstrate below for reading tarot is a nod to Waite and Smith, as it is an alchemical[12] and astrological reading, meaning that I look at different parts of each card and analyze them bit by bit according to concepts in alchemy and astrology. I offer explanations on the readings of each of the cards below in an esoteric or more social interpretation. I have also given some of the cards more modern meanings so it's easier for you to apply them to your life. Each card can imply a number of meanings, so I provide several meanings for each. Additionally in the sections below, I will talk a lot about constellations and the universe. I therefore suggest you print out star maps and learn the major constellations so you can understand what the universe looks like and receive information directly from stars and planets when you

---

10   A spiritual session is when you spend thirty to forty minutes or longer to look at a spread of tarot cards and find the dialogue there.

11   Marcus Katz and Tali Goodwin, *Secrets of the Waite-Smith Tarot: The True Story of the World's Most Popular Tarot* (Woodbury, MN: Llewellyn Publications, 2015).

12   Alchemy is a magical practice that covers a lot of subjects, but in this case it refers to using the properties of alchemical metals to decipher your tarot card meanings. Studying alchemy, especially the alchemical texts translated by Arthur Edward Waite, is a great way to further understand the hidden meanings of the cards and to learn about the soul's journey.

gaze at them. Much of the tarot is based on Greco-Egyptian knowledge, so it is also useful to look at the myths from these cultures, especially when it pertains to the heroic characters in the constellations. I will indicate to you when it's important to look at a certain myth to understand the card.

I have found that it's easiest to memorize the cards if you study them in terms of their myths and alchemical, mythological, artistic, and astrological content, and take care to analyze the emotional energy in each card and in your clients. While most tarot readers divide the deck into the suits of air (swords), fire (wands), earth (pentacles), and water (cups), I favor a more versatile style where the cards correspond to different elements and to different areas of life such as money, love, and death.

ASTROLOGY BASICS FOR TAROT

There are two major components of the astrological chart that can help you identify the qualities of people easily: the sun and the moon. When someone is born, these two astral objects are in certain zodiac constellations, and therefore the planets express themselves within the qualities of the sun and moon. People refer to this as their sun and moon sign.

I will use the terms *sun sign* and *moon sign* to describe the personalities of these cards so that it helps you respond when people ask you questions about someone during the reading. The zodiac signs are also all assigned to natural elements as follows:

- ✦ Capricorn, Taurus, and Virgo are earth signs.
- ✦ Aquarius, Libra, and Gemini are air signs.
- ✦ Sagittarius, Aries, and Leo are fire signs.
- ✦ Cancer, Scorpio, and Pisces are water signs.

The sun and moon both influence the personality and the depth and details of a person; depending on what your sun and moon signs are, you will likely behave and think certain ways.

It is also important to note that there are other planets that influence the personality, but I have left it simple here. I give descriptions of personality types for each sun and moon sign on each card.

This is also useful for associations with specific seasons and times of day when you examine a card, as the sun and moon move pretty quickly around the zodiac. For example, if you pull a card where the astrological type is a Cancer sun, that falls within the dates of June 21 to July 22. This may mean a situation will be best resolved in the summer.

USING THE TAROT

The tarot can help you in numerous ways. It can provide you with life advice and emotional support and help with casting spells. In a standard tarot deck, there are seventy-eight cards, divided into major arcana and minor arcana. The major arcana cards are labeled 0 to 21, and the minor arcana cards are divided by suits. The suits are called cups, wands, swords, and pentacles. There are ten cards, numbered ace through 10, and a page, knight, queen, and king for each suit. To easily learn, it's best to separate your piles by number and by piles of pages, knights, queens, and kings, not by the suit, then make a separate pile of the major arcana. This will give you a total of fifteen piles from which you will learn. Move at your own pace through this. Learn the minor cards first. Only work with one number or type set at a time.

TAROT MEDITATION

To connect to your cards more completely, I suggest you practice the following meditation and visualization:

Close your eyes and start to envision a very beautiful starry dark black or purple galaxy background. Once you have this background in your mind, focus on "materializing" four large sandstone tablets that will float in the space in front of you. For me, the tablets are a tan, sandy color with inscriptions on them. Focus on these cards/plates and what you see and feel for five minutes, and then exit your meditation and start to shuffle your deck. This meditation should help open your mind to messages from the divine.

THE CARDS

Below I provide my own guide for you to follow when doing readings with the Rider-Waite-Smith tarot. I found that when I first started reading the tarot, it was difficult to learn the cards without having to go online to see in-depth meanings and gain understanding. So to make it easy for you to do readings, make sure to check your intuition as to whether your card may have a more obstructive or constructive meaning that day. The energies of a card can change, so please also make sure to observe your own reactions and associations and note them in a tarot journal. I also teach you how to read each card energetically, by the colors, backgrounds, and expressions. Most tarot booklets instruct you to read the card as is if it presents itself to you upside down, but I think it is important to note for beginners that it's okay to start by just looking at the image right side up so you can hear what that card has to say and come up with your own meanings.

CUPS

Ace of Cups

The card features Columba, the constellation that is a dove, discovered in 1592. The card also features the constellation Crater (the Cup). The aces don't have sun and moon personalities because they are not about people but about processes, actions, consequences, and contracts.

Two of Cups

I believe the card focuses on business transactions and the exchange of secret knowledge. The two figures on the card don't seem to be giving off feelings of infatuation, so if it shows up in a love reading, it's not the best sign for romance. It also can mean that you may be given more responsibility at a job or in life. Corresponds with a person or people with a sun sign in Gemini and a water sign moon.

Three of Cups

The theme here is leisure and fun. This card speaks to winning something, celebrating something. The more negative meaning is doing things in excess, send-offs and goodbyes, cheating, or getting caught doing something you weren't supposed to be doing. It also can refer to drunkenness, or money that is coming, especially through betting. This person would love to be wined and dined, and possibly owns or desires a fancy car. They could also be good at storytelling. Corresponds with a person or people with the sun sign of Scorpio, a bit obsessive but not in an abusive way, and with a very happy Taurus moon who likes to wander and party.

Four of Cups

The general energy of this card is contemplative. Things may seem boring, mysterious, cruel, or hard, but that is a part of the growing process. You may have no interest in love, and education is your priority instead. If you get a really negative feeling in your gut when you pull this card, it represents existential crisis. The figure may have gotten its posture from studies of the Seated Buddha done by Smith in art school. Buddhist teachings are featured heavily in the tarot. The sun sign would be a frustrated Gemini, who maybe thinks they are smarter than others, and a Virgo moon who loves nature and writing.

Five of Cups

You have obviously done something wrong, or a bad situation is your fault. When it comes to decision making, you should take the longer route. If death is about to arrive, it will not be painful. Someone is definitely sick. They can still benefit from medicine. This also references drug issues, drunkenness, financial losses, even bankruptcy and ruin. It could also mean that you need to detox or you may have been a victim of dark magic. I would assign this person a Cancer sun sign—they would be very preoccupied and focused on losses and have a hard time maintaining work—and a Leo moon who is extra hard on themselves because they want to be super successful and well known, but may not ever meet their standards, which creates sadness. The person would have a tendency to demonstrate dramatic emotions.

Six of Cups

The reason there are flowers in the cups is because in alchemy, you can make tinctures of not only metals but also plants. Waite describes this in detail in his book about Paracelsus the physician. The card is also about gnomes, which are earth element spirits that can help you find treasure. When you pull this card, make sure to always get clarity by drawing others on top of it, as it is one of the cards that often needs a lot of clarification to get to the bottom of its deep messages.

Seven of Cups

The card overall represents versatility and life improvement. In a practical sense it is about creative abilities, immortality, and cures. The reason astrology is featured so prominently in the tarot is because the stars lead us to self-discovery, and they tell us about our origins and help us tap into brilliant ideas. Many scientists and doctors were first alchemists and astrologers, and alchemy and astrology influenced treatment and diagnosis of diseases. This card could help you coordinate effective cures and spells. The card also deals with secret identities. I would assign the figure a sun in

Scorpio and a moon in Scorpio. The person would be interested in magic and possess a lot of psychic skills as well as secret sexual desires. This would also be someone who would make a good therapist or sex worker.

Some additional history on this card: I believe both Smith and Waite immortalized themselves in this deck, and this is the card into which Waite inserted his soul. He is the dark shadow figure. The shadow also represents ghosts and spirit apparitions. The cups all contain either astrological or alchemical symbolism. Starting from the top left: The first cup features a beautiful figure sporting a curly hairstyle. A gray-cloaked figure in the second cup could be a medium or thought-reader with a fever (that red around the figure) because Waite describes that as something that happened to mediums and thought-readers. In the third cup, on the far right, is the "half snake," which is a constellation reference, to Serpens. On the bottom farthest to the left is a cup that holds metals being turned into a solution for medicine. The next cup is full of jewels and minerals, the one after that is a symbol of Corona Borealis the constellation, and then finally, the constellation Cetus is in the last cup in the bottom row.

Eight of Cups

One of the ways I like to remember this card is by looking at the golden yellow moons on the left corner. One of the moons is Earth's moon, the other is Io, one of Jupiter's moons. This is a good time to connect to Io's energy or the moon to guide you. This card also speaks to travel, moving, and fertility. Someone has left you with baggage, and they may be running away or heading away from you or ignoring you. It is a sour love card. This card also corresponds with the astrology placement of the sun in Cancer and the moon in Sagittarius.

Nine of Cups

The main theme of this card is riddles. When you pull this card, always make sure to pull clarification cards after. This one is hard to decipher and interpret on its own, and I find it's a sign to ask more questions of the client or yourself. Otherwise, someone clearly wants to bother you. They have made a point of standing in your way because they believe they are smarter than you. It is a card of enemies and adversaries, those who plot against you and try to trick or destabilize you. I would assign the figure an Aquarius sun and a Taurus moon. This card represents the presence of ghosts, or a solo show or spotlight moment.

Ten of Cups

The couple seen on the card are both actors, as both are holding up their hands and onto each other as if bowing for their show. Iris, the Greek goddess of the rainbow, is pictured here. The couple also might be irresponsible parents. I would assign the card a goofy, forgetful Pisces sun and a loving and understanding Aries moon who doesn't anger but tends to ignore responsibility and prioritize personal pleasure.

Page of Cups

This is an easy card in the sense that there is very little chaos. The water seems to be flowing normally. Interestingly, the page's clothes are much more decorative than those in many of the other cards. This is to symbolize his career as a poet or perhaps even a tailor. Humor is a part of this card, as are pleasure, sex, and the arts. This card means you will do well if you hustle and work to put yourself out there. Referring mainly to artistic careers, it can also symbolize general entrepreneurship and self-employment. The Page of Cups is fortunate and symbolizes a very interested and fast lover who wants to pursue you immediately. This is the type of lover or partner who would be obsessed with you and love you all your life. If you feel uneasy when you pull this, then read it as obsession. I also notice that the red-line drawings on the tunic are quite nervous-looking, so this could represent nervousness or even in some cases a murder or incident that involves accidental death. I would assign this card a Virgo sun, very inquisitive and open to the world, with a cheery, chatty, and social, possibly vengeful, Gemini moon.

Knight of Cups

The knight is calm as if he has put on his armor for the sole purpose of courting the person he wants. This corresponds with a Pisces sun, someone with pure intentions for love and looking to find their soul mate, but also someone who is vengeful and twisted if wronged. It also represents someone who has come back from a war and has a disability. I would assign this person a Pisces moon as well.

Queen of Cups

The queen has a Libra sun with a lot of Venusian energy and a Scorpio moon, which would make her interested in the past and in interrogating people deeply before accepting them. She is not loving.

King of Cups

This card is about bad sex or failing relationships. In astrology, the king would be an Aries or Sagittarius sun sign with a Cancer moon and a very noticeable flair, but not enough experience to be good at relationships or sex. This card symbolizes protection. This person may be talented at spell casting because they have a staff in one hand.

WANDS

Ace of Wands

This card relates to matters of sex. It is a good time to make a bank withdrawal to buy something new or invest in your future. The card is also about how you will get a new house, so it is always related to housing matters.

Two of Wands

The card features two divining rods, which are discussed in Waite's book about magic. Divining rods help people find water and precious things. The figure is a skilled diviner, astrologer, or spell caster. In terms of the zodiac, this would be a Cancer moon, with a sad Aquarius sun personality. Although this is not someone who cries a lot, it is a person who obsesses over sadness and sees life harshly and tragically sometimes.

Three of Wands

This is a timing card, referring to something that is likely to take place in the next two or three weeks. It could represent having to move when you already feel settled. I would assign this person a Capricorn sun and a Libra moon. The characteristics of the person would be that they are okay with being an asshole, and they will step on anyone who gets in their way. They like obtaining rewards and being recognized but may be a bit shallow.

Four of Wands

This card references a collective, civics, a well-organized society, and parts that come together to make a whole, as well as order, and a city founded on values and active, healthy citizens. This card also refers to invitation, welcome, and social gathering with a purpose and celebration. I would assign this card a Leo sun sign, someone who is ready to show off, intelligent and proud, with a stellar Gemini moon to make them interesting, wise, and ahead of their times.

Five of Wands

Competing for fame, attention, or money. I do not assign a sun or moon sign here because the card focuses on a group of people. Discuss group dynamics at work, socialization growing up, sibling conflict.

Six of Wands

This card reflects a Capricorn sun with Sagittarius moon, someone who comes home late and doesn't tell you where they went. Someone who prefers to be out late at night with friends instead of being home with their significant other. This would be the type of person who enjoys having more than one romance at a time, and thus it could represent the desire to be polyamorous or just plain old being okay with cheating.

However, in this case, this person would easily be exposed by rumors and gossip and nosy neighbors or friends. The card also focuses heavily on anger.

Seven of Wands

In this card you are supposed to notice the water. Even though there is only a small visible portion of the water here, we are meant to think about emotions, especially those that are deeply repressed in us. The person is obviously heated, and they are treating the issue in an immature or stupid manner that won't work. They are addressing the issue in the wrong ways and not getting to the root. This is definitely Leo sun energy, with an immature and overly frustrated Pisces moon, someone who likes to argue and create conflict and never listens to feedback. The person is doing manual labor so this is a career card. It could mean a career in sports and fitness.

Eight of Wands

No zodiac personality is assigned here since this is not a person card. This card is about relief, and as such, it provides one of the most optimistic outlooks in the deck. It means slow down and calm down; the stream and Japanese-calligraphy-style inkblots on the bottom are serene.

Nine of Wands

This is a card of the moon and Mercury, both in the placement of Virgo, and does not feature any specific sun sign. This is a person with strong values who never compromises them. This person may be religious. It can also represent head injuries, hexes, and intuition issues.

Ten of Wands

This card represents the struggle to prove yourself and bring something back or losing fear of the unknown. A Sagittarius sun who strives to solve even the most difficult of problems through magic, with a Scorpio moon who loves magic and reading and the world's many cultures. Rather than looking at this card as difficult, notice that the figure is carrying something rather light, and they look as if they possess large muscles, which means they wouldn't actually be struggling here but rather doing something more productive, like making a fire or stirring something around as his arms are wrapped around the wands in a swirling motion.

Page of Wands

Generally, the card feels dry, boring, even painful, and it appears when things are going very slowly. The page has been on a rough journey and has had some bad luck. The card appears when it is important to protect yourself and when things are about to get intense. I don't assign a zodiac combination to this card as I believe it is about the planet Venus only— particularly detriment caused by an erratic or angry Venus. Daytime on Venus lasts much longer than our day on Earth, so time is slowed on Venus; it is likely that this card is about our past and what from that may bother us. The salamander tunic represents immortality and supernatural powers.

Knight of Wands

The card is also Venusian and concerns the sexual energy of Venus. This may represent a person who takes pride in their sexuality and who has been with many other partners but is proud of it. In terms of professions, the knight may represent a political canvasser or anyone who comes to the home to provide services, like a healer or salesperson. The person would be a Libra moon who loves to read and cook and loves the home, but who also has a wild side, represented by the moon in Scorpio. The card appears when you have clean energy. The salamander tunic represents immortality, supernatural powers, and astral travel.

Queen of Wands

This card appears to those gifted in magical herbalism, biology, and birthing arts. The card is also about gender and foretells a marriage and many children. It speaks to queer and transgender love, erotic energy, and twins. The cat is an omen of bad luck, especially pregnancy losses. I would assign a Virgo moon and sun to this card. With that double Virgo energy, the person would be excellent at healing and able to withstand long hours of work and fight off bad energies.

King of Wands

This card references magical accomplishments rather than financial ones, such as gaining a position of priesthood or receiving an initiation. In my opinion the King of Wands is also an astrological card, as it represents the energies of Mars, the Red Planet, with a really sexual energy. It could mean that someone is very sexually attracted to you and could refer to great partnerships based on gender equality and bringing the best out of each other. Someone who has worked good treaties and been kind to prisoners and slaves. I would assign the king a wise Sagittarius sun sign, someone quick to protect, and a talkative Libra moon with the desire to be heard and cared for.

SWORDS

Ace of Swords

This card refers to the ability to win physical and intellectual arguments. This card is about a certain part of the sky, where the constellation Corona Borealis is located. It also represents tension in the body. It indicates that you have something to fall back on, riches or a rich family, or a really solid backup plan and an uncanny ability for your prayers to be heard. This is an easy card in terms of love. The potential suitor is pure, spiritual, romantic, and well-off. Advice should be that this is an ideal situation, and you should work to make it long term. Never let go of this person.

Two of Swords

This card indicates preparation, especially rigorous mental and physical preparation for tasks, initiations, and tests. This card is both emotional (water) and mental (thoughts). It could also refer to androgyny because the swords are crossed exactly where there would be a chest. In terms of sexual desire, it represents a kink or fetish. I would assign the card a Capricorn sun sign with a lot of endurance and a Pisces moon who sees through everything and never gets crossed or fooled. The person's energy would be very pleasant to be around because of how mature they are, to the point where they may be able to take care of many other people, not just themselves.

Three of Swords

I love explaining the deeper meaning of this card, beyond the literal heartbreak interpretation. Interpret it as a person who is a manipulative Aquarius sun and a Pisces moon. This is someone who falls in love super easily, but then the cold Aquarian tendencies makes them break hearts. Research, writing, and academics are their strong suits. This person will overcome most of their karmic debts and have a very clear soul by the end of their life. This card symbolizes a forbidden love, where two people can't live without each other and there is a lot of pain, loss, and sacrifice, but reunion in the next lifetime. Other than that, the card heavily features the metal silver so it is about money matters and beauty.

Four of Swords

One of the interesting things about this card is that at first glance it appears to be about death, and so one may feel sad or afraid at seeing it, but it has a much happier meaning in my opinion. Whenever a card is very literal, try not to read it as such, and look for the deeper meaning. This card is actually related to the sun, which we see reflected on the tomb with striking yellowish color, with an emphasis on the stained glass window. Some people see this as a Catholic symbol. I like to see it as related to ritual burials. I believe the other astrological symbol in this is Coma Berenices, which is a constellation in the northern sky. Obviously we are going to go with a serious Scorpio sun here and an Aquarius moon sign. Not a very chatty person and hard to open up, they might even be distant from family.

Five of Swords

In this card, I see a story about embarrassment. The characters feel insulted and are ashamed of themselves. This card should always be read as negative and bad luck. Contemplate whether you have done something that caused this karmically and promise not to do it again. No particular zodiac personality is associated with this card since it is a group. Avoid the blame game and focus on strategies to move forward after failure.

Six of Swords

The most typical interpretation of this card is that the characters here have been kicked out of society and have to leave, but there is more to it than that. This card features the Greek mythical figure Charon, who takes souls to the underworld on his boat, so the card represents the descent to the underworld and the afterlife. It represents a Gemini moon and Scorpio sun, a person who may be cold and stubborn and have regrets at the end of life but is able to think of the big picture and say sorry to people they hurt before death. This card is about feeling like you are strangers with someone, so perhaps ask if anyone new interests the person.

Seven of Swords

This card is about the future. I see sexual symbolism because the tents on the side are wide open and very pretty! I would assign them an Aries sun, Aquarius moon, very rebellious, even sneaky, loves sex and trouble.

Eight of Swords

This card is about self-hatred. I would assign a Taurus sun here, someone who likes to embrace the day and do a lot, not a lazy Taurus, and a Virgo moon, who is super timely. You may need or want attention. This card also means that your foundations are not solid and that you may have made a lot of mistakes. You can't fix things. This card could also refer to spiritual sight, spiritual development, possessing coveted skills, secret work, or being chosen for something. This is a card that indicates trouble with keeping money or someone who barely makes it. It flows, just not as much as they want it to. This card is associated with being barren.

Nine of Swords

Face your fear of death! We all die eventually, and the quilt in this card is a reminder that you will see your loved ones after death as they are all hanging out in the stars. This is also more of a psychological problems card, and if you are suffering, please seek out professional help. The zodiac signs I would assign here are a very difficult Aquarius moon who has suffered since childhood with a traumautized Aquarius sun who fails at love. It represents a devastated, dramatic person, or someone who dreads getting up in the morning.

Ten of Swords

The card is about invisible energies; the soul, body, and spirit; and the alchemical teachings. Furthermore, the card represents our extraordinary connection to the sublime. The card encourages you to honor your body, spirit, and soul, to remember you are special and chosen for this life, and to remember your painful life lessons. You may experience major life changes. The card has no zodiac sign correspondences; it is all about Saturn, though, as it relates to death, decay, putrefaction in alchemy and medicine, the soul's journey after death, and reincarnation.

Page of Swords

The main theme of this card is loving life and having a very good prospect in love. It is also a timing card, relaying something five to eight years in the future. I would assign a Capricorn sun—and a soft and cute, not sexy, Sagittarius moon. The person will be rich in this lifetime and will meet many important people. They will be able to become less dependent early in life. An important letter or email will arrive in the next two weeks. Don't wander too far from home. This person likely has a career connected to garments.

Knight of Swords

The key themes here are hunting and advising. The card represents someone who is in charge of feeding the family. I would assign the character a very fit Virgo sun with a Scorpio moon that makes them caring and present. Timing is important here, and it represents a fast or fleeting energy. I also see a bit of corruption in the card, so if you feel more negative about it, the card could be about bad business deals and betrayals because of money or politics, entanglements with others, or unresolved issues. The person may be a model, or in politics or the military. You may need to flee from something.

Queen of Swords

While the other queens ooze sensuality, this one focuses more on pregnancy, motherhood, and modesty and she may be of older age as well (fitting in to the archetypes of mother, maiden, and crone). The astrological makeup is Cancer sun and Scorpio moon. The queen would be someone wise in astrology, and this person likes cutting good deals in business and gives discounts if they are a business owner.

King of Swords

This card represents big business and finance professions. This card refers to someone who is open to sex, and who has an open mind to kinks and sexual fetishes, but wants to connect mentally first. This is an organized person, someone who responds to emails or calls. It also refers to someone who plays a star role in a play or movie, or a famous person. It refers to elegance and special occasions, protection, and gender roles and marriage roles being challenged. Someone with strong divination skills and someone who is a natural-born intuitive. This could be someone who interrupts a lot or is very blunt when conversations are getting boring, someone short on time and always in a rush. This is a Scorpio sun with a Gemini moon. This person would be a bit intense and loud. They would be orderly, and they would demand and expect a lot from others.

PENTACLES

Ace of Pentacles

This card indicates purity or that the person may be called to healing, especially when it comes to possessing gifts that are based in touch. This person's wealth is normal, not excessive. This person's riches are contingent on hard work. It also indicates a peace between others and simplicity in general

Two of Pentacles

The figure is dancing and joking and may be juggling. The card features the constellation Hydra in the large green infinity symbol. I would assign a lighthearted Libra sun who is viewed as young and good-looking. I would assign the Capricorn moon to this card; this person could have awesome long-term plans for themselves and feel very secure. This card is about money and concerns problems of the past, so ask about financial habits, savings, and retirement.

Three of Pentacles

The card's subject is actors, particularly those who are unknown; thus it refers to the financial tribulations associated with working in the arts.

This card is not assigned an astrological profile and focuses instead on real-life problems like taking care of kids and transportation issues, and not on any spiritual or mental advice.

Four of Pentacles

This card can refer to luck and protection and using your strong spell-casting powers to guard yourself.

Five of Pentacles

The two characters here appear out of breath and hurt as they have both "traveled" to outer space. They have safely landed on Mercury. At the top of the card is a window that appears to be stained glass, but is, if you look carefully, actually more of a tablet. (The hidden wisdom is encoded in a book called the *Emerald Tablets*.) In my opinion the character on the far left looks upon the tablet with admiration while the character on the right ignores it or is unaware of it, highlighting the fact that the tablet is "invisible." (All esoteric wisdom is hidden and can only be seen or heard by those who know.) Most Hermetic teachers believe that secret wisdom is only revealed to those who pay attention. The figure on the right is unaware of the tablet and ignores the wisdom, representing those who don't have the wisdom. The card has no astrological profile but is associated with Mercury the planet as a place.

Six of Pentacles

This card is more of a warning card, when bad energy is near. It is a Capricorn sun sign who is educated and intuitive. But use discretion as it might reference someone who is cunning and uses astrology to manipulate you. This is a financially thirsty and possibly abusive Scorpio moon. Be careful who you reveal private information to. Be careful who you choose to educate you, especially in the spiritual world, or be careful of any spirits that may be trying to come through as they may have ill intentions.

Seven of Pentacles

I believe this card corresponds with old age. The figure is holding a cane that they need to walk. It shows a disability, as well as age. The zodiac profile would be of a nicer older person who tolerates others and doesn't act superior or try to enforce rules or morality. This person could be a softer Virgo sun and an Aquarius moon that makes them futuristic and not just old-fashioned.

Eight of Pentacles

In my opinion the character represents someone who has a Capricorn sun, who is willing to work hard, and a Sagittarius moon with a lot of creative potential. On the far right is the Bodhi tree from the Buddhist tradition. The main theme here is the constellation of Caelum, which is a chisel; it is shown here as a man carving with a chisel. I believe this character is also a BIPOC person. It also refers to passion projects, careers in athletics, mechanics, architecture, or math, or a person who is a natural-born artist with great creative faculties.

Nine of Pentacles

In this card, we see a self-portrait of Smith. This character is up during the early morning, so there is a lot of sun around. The card reflects solar energy and daytime. On the left side of the card where the six gold pentacles are stacked, there is a hidden symbol—the constellation of Pictor, the Easel. An additional clue to this self-portrait are the snails located on the very bottom left of the card near her foot. In Rome, snails were used to produce art pigments that tinted an "immortal" tunic that never faded with time. Immortality is one of the goals of alchemy. I also love how elaborate Smith makes her gown in this picture, as it gives off very subtly sexy Scorpio vibes. With the golden glove, it symbolizes vaginal magic.

Ten of Pentacles

The secret symbol of the Kabbalistic tree is pictured in the ten yellow, bold pentacles. The card represents the barrier between the dead and the living and tells you there are guardian spirits watching over you. This card references compensation. The card does not have a zodiac sign assigned to it. When you feel a more negative meaning, it means a punishment.

Page of Pentacles

This is a giant. There is a great message here about money that will show up either three days later or seven to ten months later. The person is alluring and beautiful. I would assign the page a Pisces sun sign and a Capricorn moon sign.

Knight of Pentacles

This is one of the knights to be careful about. Although he may be rich in money, he always has an eerie message to deliver. The predominant tone in this card is obstructive and slightly scary. There may be a lot of incompatibility or possibly a strong karmic connection. The passion may be there, but it's not perfect. I associate the card with a Capricorn moon and the Aries sun, which can make for a difficult personality. This card symbolizes the new moon as well. The one positive thing is it signals a good time to grow some plants.

Queen of Pentacles

The constellation of Lepus is pictured here. It is the very camouflaged red rabbit in the bottom right corner. The queen is troubled here; her main downfalls are sex and love. This card makes me think of cemeteries as well, paying tribute to the dead and family history. I would assign her an Aries sun, Taurus moon. The Taurus moon loves nature and magic, while Aries prioritizes relationships over spiritual or career growth. They would not want to share, ever. Their anger would be expressed through not-so-disruptive ways such as just ignoring you, texting you instead of calling, and simply ghosting. Possibly sadness, distance, loneliness.

King of Pentacles

I see both water and earth elements being prominent here. I would say the king is also a dominant card in terms of sexuality. This is someone who likes bondage, and it represents those things you want to do in bed that you don't necessarily want to broadcast. The king himself I see as the constellation Ophiuchus, who was considered a medicine carrier, meaning he would have worked with alchemy and herbs. This constellation is home to Kepler's Supernova, which is very colorful just like the king's robe. This constellation also has twin nebulae, which may explain why we see two pairs of twin bulls. Use this to stretch your mind and plan your future thirty-plus years. When looking at a chart placement, I would assign a water moon and an Aquarius sun sign to the individual or otherwise consider Ophiuchus's influence in their life. This card also refers to water in the body, wellness, and sexual health especially for the testicles and penis. This card also refers to incredible good luck and health and can suggest the person will be well off for generations to come. This person is a great partner especially in sex, marriage, and family.

THE MAJOR ARCANA

The Fool

The main narrative of the Fool card is that there is a journey ahead the hero has to prepare for. In the whole tarot journey (that is, all the cards in order), there are a few heroic stories referenced: Boötes and Hercules are prominent. The Fool represents these travels. It suggests fortune based on bravery, forgiveness, adventure, new ideas, romance, patriotism, or liberation. The karmic issues in this person's past life may be related to immaturity, fleeing, and distraction. This card indicates the person was appreciated deeply and loved. The person may have had these past life professions: actor or poet, musician, nurse or care staff, teacher or professor, and even fashion and clothing designer. The person is gifted in clairvoyance and blessed with old age, athletics, and loves magic. This is unmistakably a soft and silly Sagittarius sun energy. The moon sign could be in Aquarius, making this person curious and excited to learn all things. I also believe that the Fool's robe is outstretched at the arms almost like wings, so I think Pegasus the constellation is represented here. (Pegasus was Hercules's magical horse.) In addition, the Fool is full of pride and an amazing LGBTQI+ icon. This card also refers to student life and college times.

The Magician

This card refers to the four elements. The association here is to the constellation Ara, the Altar. I notice this because the table the objects are on is so gorgeously painted and has a lot of detail work, so this is Smith's way of showing us the altar is important. This card also refers to romantic dates and fantasies about romance. A very hidden meaning is that it represents a sexual fantasy. Additionally the Magician's belt looks like a red-eyed snake, which is associated with temptation. It's a good card to remind us to integrate our sexual selves and to tell ourselves we are not sinners. This card further references growth phases. It is a very rewarding card. The card also represents accomplishments, education, being praiseworthy, innovation and technology, and cleanliness. The Magician represents a person with a very relaxed, intelligent, and balanced nature. The card is very romantic, but the person may be sensitive and secretive. When asked about marriage, there is a strong possibility of marriage based in true love, with a big family resulting. The person should put their energy into multiple tasks and projects to make money. In a past life, the person may have been a lawyer, farmer, spiritual teacher, healer, or doctor. On the more negative side, the person may be acting on ego, cocky and full of hubris. There may be someone watching them, someone possibly outshining them or competing with them. The Magician is absolutely a Scorpio sun and a Scorpio or Cancer moon. The infinity symbol represents substantial reality and our ability to leave our ordinary minds and mesh in with and discover the substantial reality. Waite immortalized himself in this card—he is the magician.

The High Priestess

This card is a very sexual card. It is clothed in a Virgin Mary–like manner to hide some of that symbolism. This is meant to draw away from the other obvious sexual symbolism. It is related to Venus the planet in astrology (the ground is yellow like Venus). I think the meaning of this card has to do in particular with the wetness of the vagina and ejaculations, and cunnilingus, as per the phallic pillars. The Southern Cross constellation is pictured here as a white cross located on the Priestess's chest. She studies biology, science, creation myths, religions, and the birthing arts, and so concerns things that are intimate (emotionally and sexually). I would assign the Libra sun, who is passionate about education and being right, and a sweeter Virgo moon, who cares about creatures, plants, and humans, and the environment. Someone who really wants to date. This card refers to emotions, particularly tears and sadness or grief. The other meanings are direction, reassurance, belief in self, mastership, praise, spiritual achievement, and study. This card refers to incoming bills, maturing through hardship, and life lessons.

The Empress

This card refers to sexual desires and sexual empowerment! It also refers to voting rights and equal treatment. This card could also refer to the gift of astrology, so if you're an astrologer, this is your card. The large stone picture with the Venus symbol is symbolic of all stone calendars, artifacts, stone temples, and antiques. It refers to music and partying. I find that the Empress has a Libra sun energy, with the moon placement in her chart at Taurus. She is also an LGBTQI+ icon. She is definitely a witch who respects nature. The Empress is also a CEO type, a very financially savvy person good at business and land ownership, pleasure, abundance, lusts, and orgies.

The Emperor

This card refers to property, inheritance, taxes, law, rules, jail, confinements, and punishments. It refers to someone who pillages and hoards wealth. The Emperor has Jupiter in Gemini energy, and this is the sole focus of the astrology here. This would be a person who is power thirsty and violent. The card represents the overbearing, worst days of your life. The Emperor could also represent someone who is atheistic. The Emperor represents someone who will ruin your life.

The Hierophant

The card is about the personality of someone with a moon in Scorpio, very concerned with inner growth, but not with environments or collectives. The person would have excellent meditation skills. The sun sign would be in an unpleasant, needy, and mean Virgo, which is why a lot of people consider this card unpleasant.

The Lovers

This card is about the future. The constellation of Draco is featured on the left side on the tree. (It is a snake slithering on a peach tree.) This is a Scorpio sun and Capricorn moon, someone who is always hungry. In terms of a zodiac personality profile, they would be very sensual and out about it and very flexible in terms of sexuality and gender. If you have a more negative gut feeling, the card represents losses and being broke or being ordinary. The card is about couples and couples' matters. The figure on the top appears to be giving orders, potentially representing authority figures such as religious leaders or bosses. This card also indicates disruption.

The Chariot

The main figure in this card is Thoth the Atlantean. The card features the city of Atlantis in the background. Scholars of the tarot believe that Thoth the Atlantean came to Earth from outer space to pass on his teachings, and so this card features the scene where Thoth the Atlantean touched down upon Atlantis. While Atlantis is mythical, a lot of scholars have spoken of the city, including great Greek philosophers like Plato. The two figures on the bottom of the chariot, in black and white, are sphinxes. They represent humor and also androgyny, which is why they have feminine and masculine characteristics. The Chariot here is related to future or futurism, space travel, and to new generations. I would assign the zodiac personality of a sarcastic but fun person—a Gemini moon perhaps—with some sensitivity, leadership, and good looks expressed in Scorpio sun.

Justice

The secret symbolism here is about wigs, which represent anonymity and were used in secret organizations. This card is mostly about the physical world, particularly the tribulations of bills, fines, and courts, and having to do a lot of writing. I would assign the Leo moon and the Capricorn sun, as they are argumentative but almost always right. This person would be incredibly smart and possibly speak more than one language. I also see this as a card of disability as the figure appears to be missing a leg in my opinion. This card is also related to the deaf community and using sign language. The card is about diversity!

Strength

This card represents an impending special occasion or social situation and any nerves associated with going. The card is about nervousness and anxiety. The person represented by this card may be a sun in Virgo, moon in Capricorn, with a passion for being outside, and this person usually has the urge to be a guardian and protector of others.

The Hermit

The hidden symbolism here refers to the penis and the urethra. The astrological makeup would be a Gemini sun sign and Sagittarius moon. It is someone who is well-read and values education. This is also someone who sees the bigger picture in things and resolves life problems via spiritual solutions. They would be the type to never reveal their true selves out of shame and wanting to be perceived as perfect. Definitely the card of a natural-born witch, psychic, healer, or astrologer.

Wheel of Fortune

The card is about difficulties and blockages. It also is about the learning process of life and the things outside of our control that cause us harm and difficulties. When you pull this, it is important to not focus on that which limits and instead focus on the fact that life is short and we need to enjoy it. This is the card of awakened souls, healers, those who have lived many lifetimes and remember.

In my opinion, the card is about the sun sign in Scorpio and the moon in Aquarius: someone who likes to read and knows a lot about international issues. The Wheel of Fortune represents the body, the spirit, and the soul being released from its corporeal prison.

The Hanged Man

I personally see here that this card represents someone who is agender.[13] This character reminds me of an Aquarius sun who doesn't like to be noticed but is because of their amazing mind. This strikes me as someone passionate about the sciences and reading and not interested in hanging out with others who aren't intelligent. This person has a rare quiet and meditative Aries moon combination, especially since the halo on the head is so big and bright and Aries rules over the head in astrology. People with calmer Aries demeanors are rare but

---

13 Denoting or relating to a person who does not identify themselves as having a particular gender

are extremely wise and brilliant problem solvers. I also find this card appears when your ego inflates and you become pompous. Although very wise, the hanged man card also represents a student. The card is also about exclusivity and privacy. In relationship readings, it is always about separations. Other than that, the card is solid, impressive, and mature.

Death

I have to stress that you should not get caught up in any fears when you see this card. I am a fan of looking for the bright side in all the cards, which is why I think the Death card represents creativity, the arts, theater, and being applauded for your work. It represents artistic legacies. This may be a card you see when you feel like you're missing out on things, when you're so busy in life that you don't even get to enjoy yourself. The card encourages you to be forgiving and to not let precious moments be taken from you by anger or resentment. It also encourages us to be nice to others and to look past appearances, because deep down we are all wonderful souls and we all want to be cared for. This is a card I would assign to a very old soul who can easily hear the universe's message. It represents someone artistic: a Cancer sun and a Libra moon.

Temperance

The card features the constellation Triangulum. It represents living life through calculation and excellent astrological planning. This card would be an atypical Taurus sun who never shows off or burdens people, and a Venus conjunct with the moon who has healing powers and long life. You must tend to the important things in your life and be more of a nurturing figure. This card represents moving past the student level into the teacher role. Confront things you are afraid of. For me, the Temperance card is similar to the Devil card. It challenges the strict dichotomy between good and evil, human and animal, demon and angel, and instead presents the idea of being "in between" or gray and not limited to two extremes or labels. Be easy on yourself and forgive yourself when you have judged your thoughts and actions unnecessarily.

The Devil

This card has nothing to do with demons or scary energies. In fact, it has much deeper symbolism. The card is also about reproductive rights and sexual freedom. It could represent a really cool and sexy meditation instructor or sex coach. (My personal observations are that the devil isn't a goat and this is not a goat god card, but that it shows the head of a fox. I see it with the pointy ears and the orange tinge. Foxes are featured in astrology as the constellation Vulpecula.) The card also has connections to naked witchcraft rituals. It definitely represents the constellation Taurus, which is why the two figures on the bottom have small bull horns, very feminine, fierce, and exaggerated. The card is about gender-bending and playing with gender. I also believe that one of the hidden meanings is about wisdom, represented by the owl feet on the devil figure. Thus, the card presents itself when you are ready to have a career transition or take up a new spiritual skill. It has great implications for love and for devoting yourself willingly to something hard.

The Tower

The card is about music and musical notes! This card features a Sagittarius sun and an Aries moon. This card refers to someone with a very wild life, possibly with addictions. It can signal expensive damage. It can also symbolize your life's work being ruined. It can come when you are going to have computer and tech failure. The card represents a planetary retrograde. It can symbolize a job loss or missed promotion or all your resources being taken away. It indicates that something supernatural is affecting you. The card is about music and may concern the troubles of musicians.

The Star

The large yellow star is the sun, which associates the card with the zodiac sign of Leo. I would assign the star a Taurus moon actually, someone who likes to be naked and is a healthy amount of self-absorbed, with great tastes and artistic abilities. This is also someone who can inspire crowds of fans. The card represents the future and changes in society, including bringing in new social structures and new thoughts and religions. It is teeming with optimism. Lastly I believe the card has to do with lesbianism in particular and appreciation of the body as a temple.

The Moon

The dog and the wolf in the card are the constellations Canis Minor and Lupus. This card is about personal history. I wouldn't assign it a zodiac profile. This is another card that is about desires, especially related to sexual rediscovery.

The Sun

This card features Equuleus, the Little Horse constellation. The Sun is a card of silliness, so use it to reflect on fun times. It also means you are about to receive positive attention! It also represents the contrast between the seriousness of adulthood and the carefree days of childhood. I would assign it a Cancer moon and a Capricorn sun. The card may represent someone who never changes, who wishes for elite social status, has a tendency for drama and flair, and who can hide their emotions; they may act neutral all the time and can maintain a neutral face. It can also represent being blinded or annoyed, especially when jokesters, irresponsible people, or pranksters are involved or when people in your space try to annoy you.

Judgement

Notice that this scene is not scary, especially if you compare it to artistic representations of Judgment Day. It is useful not to look at this through angelic symbolism. The angel is there to distract you from implications of necromancy.[14] Generally it represents all medical professions, which is why it has a red cross on it. I wouldn't assign a zodiac profile here as astrology isn't very relevant to the card. If this card appears, you may be under someone's spell, especially if they want you as a student or contributor to a cause.

The World

In this card the constellation Hydra is pictured. It appears when you need to connect to your cultures. The zodiac personality would be a pretty Libra moon, air sun, or water sun sign, a person whose main priority is to be considered sexy and inspiring. This card is an invitation to spend lavishly and spoil yourself. A personal connection I make to this card is that it represents body diversity, especially the plus-sized community. The card is also about the animal kingdom's messengers.

How to Work with Yerbas

Yerbas are plants that you can use in magic. I use dry yerbas in all my spells. All yerbas have incredible powers that have been bestowed upon them by the creators. Yerbas communicate to us when we hold them in our hands and we crush them, smell them, and close our eyes to receive their wisdom. All the plants listed here have told me about their properties during meditation. All plants can have flexible uses.

MAKING SPELL OILS

Brewing oils is super easy! You need to have a source of fire like a stove or bonfire—I use an outdoor stove that is attached to a grill—and a high-

---

14 The supposed practice of communicating with the dead, especially in order to predict the future, alchemy, and other magic practices of sorcery or black magic in general.

heat cauldron big enough to hold a hefty portion of oil. I make all my oils in large batches to have plenty to save for later if I have to repeat spells. Add the oil and yerbas into the cauldron and turn the heat on the lowest setting. It takes about ten minutes to build up good heat. Very carefully observe the yerbas and oil so they don't burn. At the first sign of bubbles, turn the heat off, and let the oil sit for a bit to cool off. The process should take thirty minutes or less so don't burn your yerbas. To avoid burning your oil, I suggest you watch it carefully while you brew. Pay particular attention to the smell because herbs can scorch easily with this method, so you want to make sure you never get that burning smell in your oil. After the oil is cool, place it and the yerba matter in a mason jar.

You will need one large 12-ounce glass jar for storage. The longer an oil steeps with the herb, the more potent the herbal power is. I use 7 ounces of sweet almond oil or grape-seed oil and one cup of each herb, and I add more if my intuition prompts me to do so.

The next day you can start to bottle it or add the scent (a process I call perfuming the oil) and then use it in a spell. The correct way to perfume an oil is to follow the drop amount guidelines I give you for each scent and to tailor it so that it feels good to your nose! I use both essential oils (natural) and fragrance oils (which are skin safe and used in perfumery) because they are super stimulating to the senses and last long. For each recipe I will give you the drop amount and the type of yerbas and scents you need.

BRUJERIA SPRAYS

In botanicas there are liquid spell tools that are used to perfume the body after limpias, to put in the bath, and to be used in spells. These have many names: *colonias, lociones,* perfumes, *aguas,* sprays, among others. I prefer to make them instead of buying them, but when you are short on time or money, buying them is fine. They come in almost every color and purpose.

I want to teach you how to make these on your own, though, so you can put an intention into the magical product! I call them sprays because they work with the energy of the air and stay in the air after you spray them. Sprays are used to leave a feeling of freshness and renewed energy after limpias, so you rub them gently where you would usually apply perfume. Molecules never truly die, so the best way to work with this is to imagine those microparticles filling the entire room and arranging them into "walls" to fill the room. This way the space will be charged with this energy, and all of the surroundings will be prepared for the candle-burn portion of spells.

My recipes are skin safe and don't use artificial colors, but because we are using both fragrance and essential oils, do a patch test on your skin to make sure it's okay, especially if you have sensitive skin.

To make a spell spray you need unscented witch hazel in its liquid form. This is a premade ingredient that can be found easily in stores. Witch hazel is very friendly to the skin, but the correct way to use a spray is to hold it far from your aura and body so the mist doesn't touch your face too much.

To make these sprays, you will need 3-ounce tin bottles with spray tops. Fill the spray bottle and leave a little bit of room for the oils to mix in. Add the oils according to the proportions I list (examples below), and then shake the bottle to mix all the ingredients. Smell it and make adjustments if you want more of a certain scent.

To make these extra effective, try to make them all on the full moon. It will be ready for use the next day. Sprays have many uses: Spritz them on pillows and they will do work for you while you sleep. You can spray all of your tools with a specific type, and they will automatically be turned into an object for that purpose. You can use the spray even after your candle has burned down and continue doing the work every day by spraying it before you meditate and projecting the microparticles onto the room's walls.

Spell work sprays are also very discreet and portable types of magic great for using at work or if you need to spray some Luck spray in the air at a casino, bingo game, or even a sports game. You can pack sprays in your suitcase so you don't neglect your spiritual routine during travel. The sprays can also be used on clothing. You can coordinate your outfit to what you are trying to manifest via color and lightly spray the clothes so they do something for you, not just sit on your body. You can do the same with your shoes. You can spray the shoes with a spray that represents what you want to dominate that day. All of this magic is very subtle, and so it can be done in public places. You can substitute these sprays in any other spells that ask for incense. Cool your spray in the fridge after you make it to keep it fresh.

Another thing I have done with these sprays is to create one for each of the planets (and moon) and the universe. Since we are learning a lot about the astral, you will feel called to incorporate planetary energies. Just think of what planet you would like to work under and then use its day to strengthen the spell. You will be able to magnify its energy that day and really call it in with the specific scent recipe for that planet. I also provide suggested rituals elsewhere in this book so you know when to best plan for your spells and rituals and have an idea of a good schedule for a magical practice that doesn't overwhelm you.

Sunday: Sun rules over Leo

The sun is useful for generating love and sexuality; it assists with matters of defense and protection, calling back your energy, family healing, popularity, and beauty. It is a meditation day and a day excellent for tarot and tea leaf readings.

Monday: Moon rules over Cancer

The moon is useful for all spells. It should always be used wisely in every spell you do. This is why I have recipes for three different lunar oils. It can help you get pregnant, resolve issues of the past, make money, and send energy to others.

Tuesday: Mars rules over Capricorn and Aries

Mars is useful for dealing with your enemies. Mars generally is fierce, ferocious, sexy, strong.

Wednesday: Mercury rules over Virgo and Gemini

Mercury is useful for communication and travel magic, contact with the dead, psychic improvement, healing, and mending.

Thursday: Jupiter rules over Sagittarius

Jupiter is useful for luck and large tasks or ambitious petitions, business magic, and money drawing. It is a good day for meditation and physically cleaning your altars or crystal healing.

Friday: Venus rules over Libra and Taurus

Venus is useful for relaxing, bathing, and crystal gazing. Friday is an excellent day for tarot and tea leaf readings.

Saturday: Saturn for casting the occasional unfortunate spell if you need to

Just use this day to rest unless it falls on a new or full moon. Then definitely do another spell; it's a great day for crystal healing.

Uranus

Uranus doesn't have an assigned day so you can choose one you vibe with. It is a tough planet to work with if you are not experienced, so I don't advise adding it into your magic.

Neptune

Neptune aids with feeling settled in the home, listening better, empathy, learning new languages, sending spells long distances, drawing in lovers, and general self-improvement. Work Neptune energies on Monday. Neptune rules over Pisces.

Pluto

Pluto is a planet that shouldn't be used in magic often. Pluto rules over Scorpios.

MAKING THE TINCTURES

Making glycerin tinctures is quite easy. It is always a good idea to do magic through your body, and a clever way to use the sense of taste to absorb the magical and healing properties of yerbas is to take droppers of these tinctures! These oral tinctures will help you harness the powers of the yerbas deeply and get to know them as guides.

All you need is an 8-ounce glass jar, cheesecloth, yerbas from the recipe I provide, organic raw raspberry vinegar, a little bit of filtered water, and dropper bottles. They can be used to sweeten teas or taken on their own at an amount of about three drops per day. Just charge the yerbas, place them all in the jar, and pour the food-safe glycerin over the herbs until the jar is full. Then all you have to do is shake it and leave it on your altar, making sure to provide it with reinforcing charges throughout the month as it infuses! After thirty-eight days, you can strain it into a larger mother bottle, one that you keep for later use to store all the oil you're not using. The cheesecloth is for straining the yerbas out of the glycerin. I pour the tincture to about halfway in the dropper bottle, then I add 5–6 drops of raspberry vinegar for preservation and taste and about 3–4 drops of filtered water (or more if you want a more liquid tincture, but don't use so much it takes away the plant flavor). I prefer when a tiny amount of plant matter also goes in my mouth.

All of the tinctures are good for opening the third-eye system and for connecting you with your soul, heart, and emotions. These are also great for strengthening yourself before spell work and keeping your body protected! Please ask your herbalist or medical professional if food-grade glycerin and these plants are allowed in your diet. They should all be safe to eat and consume, but depending on health conditions, birth control use, and pregnancy, it's safer to ask before trying and to be aware of your allergies.

Protection
- I cup rose
- I cup skullcap
- 2 cups white tea

To Help with Developing Powers
- I cup hibiscus
- I cup mint
- ½ cup catnip
- ¼ cup yerba santa

For Meditation
- ½ ounce spearmint
- ½ ounce lavender
- ½ ounce St. John's wort
- I ounce lady's mantle
- I ounce linden flower

For Self-Love
- I ounce calendula
- ½ ounce damiana

Relief and Spell Removal
- 2 ounces hyssop

CANDLE MAGIC

Candles are called *veladoras* or *velas* in brujeria and they are often sold as *velas preparadas*, which means they have magical oil, seeds, glitter, and yerbas added to make them an effective spell candle. After undergoing a limpia by a bruja/brujo/brujx, a person usually receives a candle to take home. It is typically a glass candle with an image, and sometimes the candle is incorporated in the limpia itself. I personally don't use glass candles a lot because they can break and create messes, and are very hard to prepare without the risk of breakage if you're not an expert.

Once you light a candle, it immediately connects to the spirit reality, and it transcends all energetic realities to do the work for you to make the spell's outcome happen. They melt into all the realities.

CANDLE COLOR

Candle color associations help you construct spells intuitively. Here are some of the most common:

- **RED:** Protection of the self and family, love, angry spells, breakup spells, ancestral spells, goal setting for the new year, success in gambling, better business and business protection, solar rituals, Jupiter rituals, pregnancy and childbirth, healing spells.

- **BLUE:** Protection from the evil eye, protection from the law, concealing yourself from others, calming spells, removal of energy cords, water spirits, Neptune magic, Mercury magic, getting ahead in life, petitions to grow your spiritual abilities.

- **BLACK:** Unfortunate spells, defensive spells, ancestral spells, sexual spells, Mars magic, Uranus magic, destruction spells, clearing haunted spaces, vehicle protection spells, slowing things down, getting rid of disease, spells that cause disease.

+ **GREEN:** To obtain luck and money, to get pregnant, to escape from difficult situations, to cause problems or cause chaos, to cast spells for the least fortunate or for social justice, to control aggression, to banish spirits, to rid yourself of memories and attachments that bother you, to save money, home cleansing and home improvement.

+ **ORANGE:** To improve schoolwork, to help children, to be creative, to do sexual magic, to make someone notice you, to win prizes and the lottery, job searches.

+ **YELLOW:** To improve meditation, solar rituals, luck, to help you correct mistakes, to help soothe the emotions, to cast unfortunate spells.

+ **GOLD:** Money and luck, to unlock ancestral gifts, to connect to your lineage, to knock down enemies and protect yourself from them, to unblock yourself, to remove unfortunate spells, long life and health, to lay down a plan for the future.

+ **PINK:** To cast love spells, to cast spells to protect your animals, to work on someone else's energy remotely, to heal, to do lunar spells, to seduce but not in a pushy way, to get dates.

+ **WHITE:** To cleanse and protect spaces, wedding day spells or wedding planning spells, to clear paths and make opportunity, to improve your physical appearance, to stay young, beauty spells, spells to be cast on children or babies.

+ **PURPLE:** To receive visions, to receive spiritual messages, to honor the nighttime, to represent the night sky, to elevate yourself to a new level, goal setting, new year spells, protection.

+ **SILVER:** To get pregnant, lunar spells, spells for the new year, to correct a mistake, to seal someone's mouth shut if they gossip or talk about you inappropriately, to make you famous or noticeable, money, luck, protection.

CANDLE SHAPES

I favor wax shape candles in my work because for several reasons. They come in many cool shapes and you can choose the best one for your spells using my suggestions or your intuition. Later on in the book I will give you specific types of candles to buy, but if you can't find them at your local botanica, yerberia, or mercado, then just use any candle that your intuition draws you to that corresponds with your goal. Preparing candles is simple. You need a craft metal sheet (tin or copper is best). This will serve as your "mixing" plate to roll the candles on. The metals are powerful tools of alchemy. Pour a dropper or two of spell oil on the candles, then roll them in pinches of the yerbas I indicate you use in a spell. Keep it light so that you don't have a very volatile flame. While you do this, focus a lot of energy on the outcome you're trying to make happen. Burn the candles on a glass or ceramic plate or a metal tray to avoid fires. The preparation of the candle should take about one hour and be done the same day the spell is cast, incorporated into a ritual that lasts a total of two hours or more.

Always write the following down with paint and paintbrush when you do a spell on your candle-burning plate, using dragon's blood ink on a piece of papyrus or parchment, for your records.

I cast a spell upon my life

[Your full name]

[Your birth date]

[Your address]

CANDLE AND CRYSTAL SPELLS
FOR COMMON PROBLEMS

The following crystal/candle spells have very specific instructions, so read them carefully and execute them exactly as listed, placing each crystal as described on yourself while lying down. You can gather up all these sets of crystals and put them in a special deep purple or bright red velvet bag to continuously work with them.

TO HELP WITH ADDICTIONS

Always pair everything with mental health therapy.

- **MOOKAITE:** Above the head
- **SCOLECITE:** In the bony area between the eyebrows
- **SUNSTONE:** In the middle of the neck
- **RUBY:** In the middle of the upper chest
- **WHITE OPAL:** Right above the belly button
- **ROOT BEER CALCITE:** Under the belly above the underwear line
- **CHINESE TURQUOISE:** Three pieces at the feet

The spell candles to support this should be pink and white, prepared with the yerbas wormwood, mint, jasmine, and epazote. Use a tin craft sheet[15] to roll these candles in New Moon oil, and use New Moon spray for the room and bedding.

TO HELP THE CLIENT MANIFEST MONEY AND JOBS AND TO OPEN CHANNELS OF LUCK

* **PYRITE:** Above the head
* **LEPIDOLITE CRYSTAL CLUSTER:** At the top of the nose
* **AMETHYST:** At the mouth or at the chin
* **GOLDEN LABRADORITE:** Middle of the chest
* **TOURMALATED QUARTZ:** Right above the belly button
* **BLACK TOURMALINE:** Under the belly right above the underwear line
* **ARAGONITE FROM CHIHUAHUA:** At the soles of the feet

The spell candles for this spell should be four stuffed silver taper candles and four stuffed purple candles using star anise and blessed thistle. Use Luck oil, Money oil, Full Moon spray, Luck spray, and Money spray. Place them all in a circle and burn after this crystal meditation on a full moon.

TO IMPROVE MEMORY AND STUDY HABITS

* **MEXICAN AZURITE:** Above the head
* **SMOKY QUARTZ:** Tip of the nose
* **CINNABRITE:** On the throat
* **PURPLE CHAROITE:** On the center of the chest
* **DALMATIAN JASPER:** Above the belly button

---

15 A slice of thin metal that can be reused to roll the candles in. Tin was used in the arts and in ceremonial altars made for processions in my motherland, and is also important in alchemy.

- **BUMBLEBEE JASPER:** In the middle of the legs
- **SNOWFLAKE OBSIDIAN:** At the soles of the feet

The candle used here should be a blue skull candle stuffed with damiana and goldenseal. Use Academic Success oil and Student Life spray. Burn the candle on a Saturday.

FOR HEALING FRIENDSHIPS AND FAMILY RELATIONSHIPS

- **BLUE AVENTURINE:** Above the head
- **PINK DOLOMITE FROM ARKANSAS:** The throat area
- **RHODONITE:** The throat area below the last crystal
- **PINK OPAL:** Chest in the middle of the clavicles
- **BLUE LACE AGATE:** Above the belly button
- **RAINBOW OBSIDIAN:** Right above the underwear line
- **GREEN NICKEL MAGNESITE FROM AUSTRALIA:** At the ankles

For this spell use five small pink taper candles and New Moon spray, then roll them in fine coconut flakes. Burn them on a Friday early evening.

LUNAR SPELLS
Use this to invite the moon's beauty to help with positive perceptions and images of self and issues of love, and to draw in the power of the moon to any spell you want.

- **GREEN TOURMALINE IN MATRIX:** On the top of the head
- **WHITE MOONSTONE:** On the nose
- **LAPIS LAZULI:** On the throat
- **ZEBRA JASPER:** Below the breast line
- **PINK CALCITE:** Right below the belly button

- **LEPIDOLITE:** On the genital area
- **YELLOW TOPAZ:** At the feet

Anytime you want to do a spell that involves the moon it is important to use the color silver. So for this use any silver candle stuffed with skullcap, boldo, and lavender. Use the moon oils and moon sprays.

FOR GENERAL EXHAUSTION PREVENTION

- **BERYL:** On the forehead near the scalp line
- **BROWN TIGER'S EYE:** At the mouth
- **BROWN MOONSTONE:** At the throat where it meets the chin
- **AMAZONITE:** Center of chest
- **GREEN MOONSTONE:** Stomach
- **HEMATOID QUARTZ:** Genitals
- **CITRINE:** At the feet

The candle should be a red skull candle, stuffed and sealed with plantain leaf, rue, lemongrass, boneset, and elecampane. Use Protection oil, Trauma and Grief Relief oil, Energy Increase oil, Jupiter spray, and Mars spray.

FOR EXHAUSTED PARENTS OR CARETAKERS, THOSE WHO TAKE CARE OF OTHERS, AND EMPATHY FATIGUE

- **BERYL:** On the forehead near the scalp line
- **BROWN TIGER'S EYE:** At the mouth
- **BROWN MOONSTONE:** At the throat where it meets the chin
- **AMAZONITE:** Center of chest
- **GREEN MOONSTONE:** Stomach

* **HEMATOID QUARTZ:** Genitals
* **CITRINE:** At the feet

The candle should be a red skull candle, stuffed and sealed with plantain leaf, rue, lemongrass, boneset, and elecampane. Use Protection oil, Trauma and Grief Relief oil, Energy Increase oil, Jupiter spray, Mars spray, Protection spray, and Energy Increase spray.

TO HEAL AFTER THEFT, AUTO ACCIDENTS, FIRES, OR OTHER TRAGEDIES

This will help draw out the energies from these difficult situations.

* **CHALCOPYRITE:** Right above the head
* **AMETRINE:** In between the eyes
* **BLUE OBSIDIAN:** The middle of the throat
* **BLOODSTONE:** At the stomach above the belly button
* **CHRYSOPRASE:** Belly line right above the underwear
* **LEOPARD SKIN JASPER:** Right above the genitals
* **GARNET:** Right below the butt

Use a white candle shaped like a pyramid or a circle. Stuff the candle with St. John's wort and sprinkle it with marshmallow root powder. Use Protection oil and Limpia oil. Use Protection spray and Venus spray, Mercury spray, Full Moon spray, and Solar spray.

FOR WHEN YOU NEED TO RELEASE THE PAST

* **CARIBBEAN CALCITE:** At the forehead
* **WATERMELON TOURMALINE:** At the top of the nose
* **WHITE JADE:** At the throat
* **CHAROITE:** At the breasts
* **DARK RED JASPER:** Above the belly button

+ **SHIVA LINGAM:** At the belly button
+ **MEXICAN CRAZY LACE AGATE:** At the feet

For this use a bright blue pillar candle. Stuff the candle with eucalyptus and chamomile and use New Moon oil and Limpia oil. Use New Moon spray and Saturn spray and sprinkle silver glitter on top.

FOR PEACEFUL SLEEP

+ **OCEAN JASPER:** Above the head
+ **CLEAR CRYSTAL QUARTZ:** At the forehead
+ **LABRADORITE:** At the throat
+ **BLUE TIGER'S EYE:** At the sternum
+ **GARNET:** Above the belly button
+ **GREEN AVENTURINE:** Below the belly button
+ **ZOISITE WITH RUBY:** At the feet

Use a human figure candle in black or a black skull candle and stuff it with orange peel, poppy seeds, and lavender. Use Limpia oil, Health oil, and Protection oil. Build a bedside altar and burn it there. Use Health spray, Limpia spray, and Protection spray.

TO SAVE UP MONEY FOR A BIG OCCASION

+ **GREEN FLUORITE:** At the forehead
+ **EMERALD:** At the bottom of the nose
+ **ONYX:** At the neck
+ **RUBY IN GRANITE:** At the breasts
+ **RAINBOW OBSIDIAN:** At the belly button
+ **SMOKY QUARTZ:** At the knees
+ **PEACH CALCITE:** At the feet

Use a gold candle and a brown candle. Stuff the candles with blessed thistle, cinnamon, allspice, bay leaves, and a sprinkle of brown sugar. Use a gold thread to tie both candles together. On the gold candle, write a petition to manifest more money. On the brown candle, write a petition to help you save and not have unexpected expenses. Sprinkle them with gold glitter. Use Luck oil, Money oil, and Energy Increase oil. Use Luck spray, Money spray, and Energy Increase spray.

TO HELP MANIFEST MONEY AND JOBS AND TO OPEN CHANNELS OF LUCK

- **PYRITE:** Above the head
- **LEPIDOLITE CRYSTAL CLUSTER:** At the top of the nose
- **AMETHYST:** At the mouth or at the chin
- **GOLDEN LABRADORITE:** Middle of the chest
- **TOURMALATED QUARTZ:** Right above the belly button
- **BLACK TOURMALINE:** Under the belly right above the underwear line
- **ARAGONITE FROM CHIHUAHUA:** At the soles of the feet

The candles for this spell should be four stuffed silver tapers and four stuffed purple candles using the herbs star anise and blessed thistle. Use Luck oil and Money oil and Full Moon spray, Luck spray, and Money spray. Place them all in a circle and burn after this crystal meditation on a full moon.

LIFESTYLE SPELLS

SEND LOVE TO YOUR ENEMIES SPELL

This spell is used purposefully to fight off hexes and fix the energy of your enemies. I like to share this spell because I prefer to send love to my enemies instead of multiplying the bad feelings! This allows you to create positive karma that will fill your life with better things and help keep you safe from hexes.

You will need:

- 1 rainbow candle
- Permanent marker
- Jasmine
- Calendula
- Green tea leaves
- Lemon

Write the name of each enemy and their addresses and birthdays if you have it on the candle. Dress or stuff the candle with the yerbas and then burn!

Incantation:

May a pool of effortless, divine healing energy be directed at all of my enemies. May this candle turn all your unfortunate energy and jealousy into love! [Then state the name of each enemy]

When you cast this spell, place the lemon on your altar so it absorbs any negative and sour energies that your enemies are sending you.

BREAKUP SPELL

I have a soft spot for this spell because it was my great-grandmother's specialty. My mom used to tell me stories about how neighbors would constantly come to my great-grandmother's advising room to request breakup spells! These spells are frowned upon by some brujx, but I have cast them many times. The goal of this spell is to break up a couple. Candles for breakup spells are sold in the physical shape of two people with their backs turned in anger. The combination of catnip and slippery elm will make the lovers forget each other. Catnip can be used to cast chaotic, messy energy into the relationship! Butcher's broom will cause issues in the home and arguments.

You will need:

- 1 thick black candle
- Slippery elm
- Catnip
- Butcher's broom
- Wax stick
- Wax seal
- Break Them Up oil

Carve or write the names of the people you want to break up on the candle with their birth dates if you have them. Prepare the candle with the yerbas by poking a hole that is about one-third of an inch deep into the bottom of the candle. Fill the hole with the yerbas, about a pinch of each. Seal the hole with the wax stick by melting it on the hole, and then use the seal to make it closed. Drip 3 to 4 drops of oil on the candle.

Say the following magic words:

They may be together now, but this will end. Make them argue, make them bitter, make them break up, spirit friends! Let ___ [the person you want for yourself] be mine to claim!

FIGHTING INJUSTICE SPELLS

These spells can help you do your part to fight the white supremacist colonial patriarchy.

Free Someone from Prison Spell/Abolition

* 1 black key-shaped candle in any color
* 1 large dark purple candle
* Lemongrass
* Wax stick
* Wax seal
* Protection oil
* Luck oil
* 1 kunzite crystal
* The Chariot card

Prepare the candles with the yerbas by poking a hole that is about one-third of an inch deep into the bottom of the candle. Fill the hole with the yerbas, about a pinch of each. Seal the hole with the wax stick by melting it on the hole, and then use the seal to make it closed. Drip 3 to 4 drops of oil on the candle.

Gather all the objects, including the crystal and tarot card, and light the candles during a full moon in the night after 1 a.m.

Help Someone Gain Victory in an Election

* Health oil
* Election Help oil
* Luck oil
* Full Moon oil
* Mars spray
* Moon spray
* Venus spray
* 3 pieces of lapis lazuli

- 10–13 short light-blue candles
- 1 large red candle
- Calendula
- Shredded pieces of money
- Gold glitter
- Silver glitter
- Dirt from in front of the state capitol or city hall

Cut the calendula flowers into small even pieces. Add oil to the candles. (You can use aluminum foil to prep all the candles so you don't make a mess, and aluminum is valuable in that it adds to the magic power.) Roll the candles in the yerbas, dirt, oils, glitter, and money.

Spray the surface of your altar with all the sprays. Spray the room and do your spray activation. Burn all the candles at once. Place the lapis lazuli on the altar space for an added effect. Cast the spell on a Saturday anytime.

SURGERY AND MEDICAL PROCEDURE SUPPORT SPELL

Performing a spell during a health crisis or a surgical or medical procedure can help the person who is suffering recover or even save their life. While I can't guarantee that any spell will delay what the universe has decided about someone's fate, this type of spell usually helps the person afflicted feel less nervous going into a medical procedure.

You will need:

- 4 brown taper candles
- 1 white candle
- 1 Sharpie
- Health oil
- Medical Support, Health, and Healing spray
- Arnica
- Lungwort

- Motherwort
- Comfrey leaf
- 1 herb that supports the specific surgery or medical need (For example, I would use skullcap for brain surgery, and roses are great for cosmetic procedures and plastic surgery. I have provided you with an alphabetical guide of yerbas as an appendix that you can look to for inspiration for this spell.)

Write your name or the person's name and short intentions on each candle. Roll all the candles in the oil and spray. Roll the candles on the arnica, lungwort, motherwort, comfrey leaf, and your herb of choice. After they are rolled in the herbs and oil, stand them all up in a circle and burn them.

Incantation:

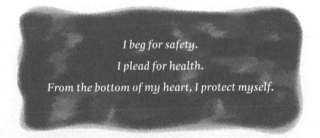

I beg for safety.
I plead for health.
From the bottom of my heart, I protect myself.

ENEMY MAINTENANCE

The purpose of this jar spell is to keep your enemies away from you and to prevent their spells from ever getting to you. The idea is that they will be stuck or be prevented when they try to do bad things to you. Note that this spell doesn't harm the enemy unless you want it to—it only stops them from hurting you. The train track dirt here is a warning of some sort to them to stop hurting you and to symbolize your dominance over them.

You will need:

- List of your enemies on paper
- Pictures of your enemies (printed in about 1-inch size)
- 1 12-ounce clear jar
- Plenty of train track dirt (Dirt from where a train passes, enough to place in a jar and have names buried in it. Gather about 5 cups of this to store for later use.)
- 3 drops of merlot or brown vinegar
- 1 small piece of three-ply twine twisted into eight knots
- Bugs (Scavenge outside for them and make sure they have had a natural death. Usually small spiders, moths, ants, and winged creatures work great. Thank them for living a good life and serving you now.)
- 40 cloves

For this spell it is okay to channel rage and passion in a firm voice. Incantation:

> *Enemies! Beware of me! I dominate you, I bury you, ____*
> *[say their names], you may never be able to harm me!*
> *I stop you, ____ [say their names], from doing me any harm.*
> *I bury our feud. I bury your name and picture so you may be*
> *stopped from doing me any harm or casting hexes, jinxes,*
> *curses, and unfortunate spells at me! You can*
> *never fucking touch me, and this I command!*

Make the jar starting with train track dirt at the bottom in a half-inch layer. Place the names and pictures of each enemy in the glass. Bury their names within the dirt, and then leave a bit of space for the cloves at the very top. Crush the bugs and also add them in on top. Carefully drip three drops of water and three drops of merlot on top. Seal the jar and then keep this in a place that gets no light at all (a dark closet or basement is perfect). Take it out every two full moons to strengthen the charm and refresh the protection or to add new enemies.

BASIC ANCESTRAL MAGIC

Your ancestors are called your *antepasados,* and communicating with them can be simple and helpful. Gather as many photos of your ancestors as you can as well as a family tree, if available. (You can do this by asking for names and histories from someone in your family and trying to go back as many generations as you can, doing ancestral research online, or taking a DNA test.) It is also okay not to see certain family members; this may mean they want to stay at rest or don't get along with you. If you feel off, then don't connect to them. I keep the pictures of my ancestors I most like and pull them out whenever I feel like communicating.

I set up a comfortable and loving vibe with my altar and then just sit in front of it with crystals, pictures, candles, and objects that have been handed down to me to connect deeply. (Old objects and family heirlooms do wonders.) I concentrate on the following phrase: "My ancestors are with me." I keep notes of what energies and encounters I experience. We all have a lot of ancestors, and so over time you will learn which spirits are drawn to you and are likely to help you.

SPRAY AND OIL RECIPES

To make these the best for you, customize the fragrance according to your nose. I will give you suggestions as to how to blend, but you can always add more or less than the recipes suggest. Use the same proportion of fragrance ingredients in both the oil and the spray. Most of the time you will use an entire bottle of essential oil or fragrance oil making a spray or oil. All spray recipes are made in a 3-ounce bottle. All oils will be in 8-ounce sizes. Refer to "Brujeria Sprays" (page 73) for basic instructions on how to make both.

Energy Increase/Energy Change Oil and Spray
- 3 ounces slippery elm
- 1 ounce avocado leaves
- 1 ounce olive leaf

For the fragrance:
- 60–70 drops geranium essential oil

Medical Support, Health, and Healing Oil and Spray
- 15 guarana pods
- 8 ounces grape-seed or sweet almond oil

For the fragrance:
- 35 drops bergamot essential oil
- 20 drops geranium essential oil
- 12 drops freesia fragrance oil

Job Drawing
- 8 ounces sweet almond or grape-seed essential oil
- 2 ounces cat's claw

For the fragrance:
- 30 drops turmeric essential oil
- 10–15 drops honeysuckle essential oil

This should smell heavily of the turmeric, but to tone it down and make it complex, I add the honeysuckle to make it very fresh and not just spicy.

Limpia
- 2 ounces linden flower
- 1 ounce mint

- 1 ounce rose
- 1 ounce chrysanthemum
- 60 drops bergamot essential oil
- 30 drops lavender essential oil

Luck Spray and Oil

- 3 ounces yucca root
- 50 drops French vanilla essential oil

New Moon

- 8 lotus root slices
- 12 bay leaves
- 20 drops geranium essential oil
- 60 drops lemon essential oil

Protection Spray and Oil

- 1 ounce boldo leaves
- ½ ounce dandelion root
- 8 ounces grape-seed or sweet almond essential oil

For the fragrance:
- 50–60 drops coconut fragrance essential oil (go heavy on this)

Saturn

- 30–40 drops amber fragrance essential oil
- 2 ounces dried orange peels
- ½ ounce wormwood

Solar Oil

- 2 ounces raspberry leaf
- 25–30 drops coriander essential oil

Sex Worker/Sexual Healing

- ✦ 40 drops geranium essential oil
- ✦ 40 drops freesia essential oil
- ✦ 80 drops bergamot essential oil

Spell Break

- ✦ 2 ounces of boldo leaves
- ✦ 60 drops nag champa fragrance oil

Stop Gossip

- ✦ 2 ounces devil's claw root
- ✦ 1 ounce eucalyptus
- ✦ 75–80 drops freesia fragrance essential oil

Trauma and Grief Relief

- ✦ 1 ounce motherwort
- ✦ 1 ounce borage
- ✦ 8 ounces grape-seed or sweet almond essential oil

For the fragrance:

- ✦ 50 drops lemongrass essential oil

Universe Spray and Oil

- ✦ 3 ounces *abre camino*
- ✦ 75 drops eucalyptus essential oil
- ✦ 30 drops neroli essential oil (add more if you can't distinguish between the neroli and lemon)
- ✦ 60 drops lemon essential oil

Full Moon/Tlazolteotl

- ✦ 1 ounce wormwood

- 40–50 drops cedarwood essential oil
- 60–75 drops grapefruit essential oil

Waning Quarter Moon/Tochtli

This occurs when the moon is growing, right after it's new.

- 2 ounces fig leaf
- 60 drops lavender essential oil
- 20 drops white musk essential oil
- 80 drops mandarin essential oil
- 20–30 drops spearmint essential oil

Add the spearmint oil last and in small amounts because it tends to overpower every other scent if you're not careful.

Waxing Quarter/Sad Release/Mayahuel

This occurs right after the full moon when the moon starts to darken and looks like it's cut in half. I specifically named this Sad Release so it can get you through rough moments with lots of love.

- 3 ounces chaparral
- 30–40 drops ylang-ylang essential oil

Money

- 3 ounces blessed thistle
- 20–25 drops nag champa fragrance oil

Last Long

This should be used to make spells last for longer periods of time and with the spells you do most often.

- 1 ounce damiana

- 2 ounces lemongrass
- 50 drops green musk fragrance essential oil
- 30 drops white musk fragrance essential oil

Pay Me Back

This should be used as an aid for paying bills and decreasing debt and getting payments from those who owe you money.

- 2 ounces marshmallow root
- 1 High John the Conqueror root
- 75–80 drops strawberry-scented essential oil

Receive Messages Oil

- 2 ounces hydrangea root
- 2 ounces dandelion leaf
- 60 drops lavender essential oil
- 30 drops cardamom essential oil

Haunted Home Help

This should be used to help clear attachments in living spaces.

- 3 ounces arnica
- 60 drops wisteria fragrance essential oil

Academic Success Oil and Student Life Spray

- 2 ounces horehound
- 75 drops green apple fragrance essential oil
- 75 drops coconut fragrance essential oil

Venus

- 3 ounces uva ursi
- 75 drops lemon verbena fragrance essential oil

Jupiter

- 3 ounces chamomile
- 2 ounces agrimony
- 40 drops green Egyptian musk essential oil
- 10–20 drops jasmine essential oil

Stay Away Racist

- 3 ounces lemon verbena
- 75–80 drops pure tea tree essential oil

Mercury

- 3 ounces rosemary
- 75–80 drops lime essential oil

Uranus

- 2 ounces hops flowers
- 60 drops sweet orange essential oil
- 60 drops tangerine essential oil

Neptune Spray

- 3 ounces elderflower
- 60–75 drops sweet pea essential oil

Mars Spray

- 1 ounce licorice root
- 10–20 drops ginger essential oil

Ginger essential oil is super pungent, so I like to make this spray on the lighter side, using around fourteen drops of the oil. Adjust according to your own preferences.

Election Help/Political Activism

- 1 ounce calamus root
- 1 ounce roses
- 1 ounce yarrow
- 40–50 drops camphor essential oil

Break Them Up

- 3 ounces stinging nettle
- 40 drops fir needle essential oil

Love Attraction

This is used to make you deeper and more soulful, not to force love.

- 8 cacao beans
- 1 ounce dried strawberries
- 1 ounce black tea
- 75 drops clary sage

Come Back to Me Oil

- 1 ounce dittany of Crete
- 60 drops freesia essential oil
- 40 drops jasmine essential oil

SANTA MUERTE

Before I proceed to tell you about Santa Muerte, I should begin by stating that I see Santa Muerte as an actual part of the LGBTQI+ community, and so I worship her/them as such. She/they[16] has made it

---

16   By referring to Santa Muerte as she/they, I am categorizing Santa Muerte's gender identity as both woman and as someone outside of the gender binary who would use a pronoun like they/them instead of she/her.

clear to me that she/they is queer and this is important in getting to know her/them and in helping you learn about the queer community. The reason I use she/they as pronouns for Santa Muerte is because she/they has a woman's energy, and she/they is also a shape-shifter goddess (takes on a lot of forms and shapes) so the pronoun *they* represents the part of Santa Muerte that is a nongendered or genderqueer deity.

Santa Muerte is incredibly loving and protective of her/their children, LGBTQI+ or straight. She/they will guard over anybody who comes to her/them with good intentions and love, regardless of their identities or marginalized professions or social classes. Sometimes people are born with her/them as a spirit guide, and so she/they reveals herself/themselves via visions and asks them to become a devotee. She/they can also be acquired as a spirit guide if you are truly drawn to her/them and that is correct for your lifestyle. After reading this section, you should make note of what your initial feelings are, and then ask the tarot cards if this is good for your spiritual growth.

Now into her/their background: Santa Muerte means "holy death," but she/they is much more than just a deity that represents the end of it all! In my homeland there were many death deities: Mictlantecuhtli, Mictecacihuatl, Tlaltecuhtli, and even Tezcatlipoca, so the worship of Santa Muerte exists there because of this. She/they is not just involved with the reality of the dead, but also with the greater universe. She/they heals those who are connected and lends her/their healing powers to those who want to use them for curing and blessing people. When you connect to her/them, she/they will help you improve your spell work and your reading skills. She/they is a deity we can associate with old age and the wisdom of being an elder, with motherhood and midwifery, with warriors, with the Earth and its plants and animals, with the afterlife and reincarnation, and with beauty and love, funerals, partying and joy, the soul's journey after death, spell work, divination, and *curanderismo*.

Entering into a relationship with her/them should be honored as a special occasion. You are *not* selling your soul or making a deadly pact with her/them when you start your worship. You should note that she/they does prefer that you worship her/them often. Time is very important to her/them. Although it doesn't have to be daily or feel restrictive like the way the Catholic Church promotes worship, you should honor her/them with deep contemplation two to three times a week as well as perform mini rituals and offerings to really keep her/them happy. I suggest you always have at least one candle with her/their image on it and try to never neglect lighting the candle and connecting to her/them daily. There is a simple way to make sure you don't upset her/them, and that is to show up with love. Be willing to receive her/their guidance and teachings and to give her/them a cold glass of water every single day to make sure her/their thirst is quenched. While she/they would ideally like it if you keep her/them around forever and pass her/them down to your grandchildren, she/they will not punish you for being imperfect! She/they understands that life can get a bit hectic and emotional, so if you need to take care of yourself first, and not make her/them a priority because of your mental health, family, work, or travel, you are allowed to do this.

The practice of worshipping her/them will be more successful if you use your imagination and intuition as you learn how to work with her/them for spells. Don't worry too much about the "rules" of practicing. (It's just important not to appropriate her/them or to use her/them to make money that should be going to BIPOC folks who have preserved this knowledge and deserve to reap all the benefits of this.) Spell work, music and dance, the outdoors, and oral worship[17] are important to this practice. In the pages that follow I provide my own channeled words to use to activate your relationship to her/them and to build up to asking her/them for things.

---

17 I really want to stay away from the use of the terms *prayer* or *mantra* to bring this into a less religious and less appropriative context.

I give all this knowledge to you because Santa Muerte has been an incredible guide for me. She/they has helped me through really hard times. I always go to her/them when I feel that all is going wrong, and she/they consoles me. Although as a saint, she/they is a symbol of colonialism in some ways, many practitioners of brujeria feel connected to her/them, and she/they is a good guide for those looking to try this practice. Further, there is almost no botanica, yerberia, or mercado that won't have her/their candles and spiritual tools widely available.

CONNECTING TO SANTA MUERTE

The best way to connect to Santa Muerte is by using oral worship in a series of seven days. Each day you will say specific channeled words to connect to her/them, meditate, and write down your observations of what you feel. I will also teach you the channeled words of worship I have made up to replace the hetero-patriarchal prayers that are used in Santa Muerte worship circles. My prayers to Santa Muerte are empowering and LGBTQI+/feminist-friendly channeled words, as I know that Santa Muerte would not want to be worshipped solely through patriarchal language. These prayers replace traditional Catholic recitations.

You also don't have to pay her/them any money to begin your worship practice and you don't need to receive an initiation, baptism, or special ritual done by a professional before you start to worship or ask her/them for things.

If she/they asks you to mark the relationship milestone with a special ceremony, there are practitioners who can help with this. Don't pay in excess for any of these ceremonies. It is common for scammers to make you believe you need to pay them for things or give excessive donations, but this is *not* something that Santa Muerte requires. Money is a nice gift if you have dollars to spare, especially when you go to a temple, shrine, public service, or group reading dedicated to her/them. The reason that she/they does not require you to go through a special process of initiation or baptism is because she/they is here to serve us all and wants us to have no barriers to learning and to growing close to her/them.[18] She/they understands all languages, which is part of why she/they is worshipped worldwide.

Calling her/them by other names is also a way to connect to her/them in a manner that is not just based in Catholicism. She/they has been referred to by these names: La Flaquita,[19] La Patrona/La Patronx,[20] Abuela/Abuelx,[21] Madre,[22] and various names after her/their cloak colors.

THE UNIVERSAL MAGIC WORDS OF SANTA MUERTE

The Universal Magic Words of Santa Muerte are a set of worship words. They were originally written in Spanish by me, and I encourage you to use the Spanish prayer as it works better than English in contacting her/them, but I have provided the translations in English in case you don't speak or understand Spanish.

Gran Madre Muerta,
Gran Madre Tierra,
Madre Ancestral!
Tú que eres Protectora!

---

18 The baptism done in Catholicism has been adapted into the Santa Muerte traditions. Water, prayers, and Afro-Indigenous traditions are involved. It is not just done to children, though, but is more commonly offered to adults who want to honor her/them and join a "family" of Santa Muerte children under what is called a *padrinx* or *madrinx* (a sponsor). I personally have no associations with any Santa Muerte family.
19 The bony one
20 An empowering term that means "boss" or "badass"
21 Grandmother and grandparent
22 Mother

Nuestra madre guerrera!
Libranos y Sananos!
Enseñanos los caminos y Abrenos las puertas
de la oportunidad.
Aunque fallas tenga yo, por favor aceptame, Santa Muerte!

✦

Oh my Great Dead Mother!
Oh great mother of the Earth!
Oh great ancestral mother!
Liberate us and heal us,
protector, warrior mother!
Show us the pathways and open the doors to opportunity.
Please accept me, flaws and all, Santa Muerte!

THE UNIVERSAL MAGIC WORDS OF SANTA MUERTE II

Santa Muerte, todapoderosa/todapodorosx,
Tú Tienes un lugar permanente en mi casa y en mi corazón.
Te ruego por una vida larga y alegre y una muerte justa, preciosa,
facil. Quedate conmigo, Santita, hasta mis ultimos días!

✦

Santa Muerte, all-knowing and all-powerful,
You have a permanent space in my home and my heart.
I ask for a long and happy life, and a fair, precious, easy death.
Stay with me, Santa Muerte, until my final days!

Say the Universal Magic Words of Santa Muerte in the morning and the Universal Magic Words of Santa Muerte II at night as many times as you feel inspired. Additionally, make sure to recite every week the special prayers below to complete each day's oral worship. Completing these full seven days of oral worship isn't always necessary, but it is very useful as a beginner, and it is critical when you are going through a hard time or when you have been neglectful and need to show Santa Muerte more devotion.

MONDAY: THE RECITATION TO OPEN UP
TO SANTA MUERTE AND TO FEEL HER/THEM

Say it ten to thirteen times at night near her/their candle.

Aquí en mi altar,
aquí, en mi hogar,
me encuentro contigo, Santísima!

✦

Here with my altar,
here in my home,
I encounter you, Santísima!

TUESDAY: THE RECITATION TO HAVE SANTA MUERTE ENCIRCLE YOU WITH A RING OF PROTECTION

Say it ten to thirteen times at night.

Mi favorita!
Mi favorita!
Mi favorita señorita!
Hoy le pido
Hoy le pido
Su círculo de protección!

✦

My favorite!
My favorite!
My favorite señorita!
I ask you, I ask you to encircle me
with your ring of protection!

WEDNESDAY: THE RECITATION TO BECOME STRONG AND BE ABLE TO PROTECT YOURSELF

Say it eight times at night.

Hoy le pido gran bruja vieja, que me cubra
con su manto de protección!

✦

> *My beautiful old bruja, please cover me with*
> *your cloak of protection!*

THURSDAY: THE RECITATION TO
BREAK THROUGH YOUR BARRIERS

Say it ten to thirteen times at night.

> *Librame librame, madre mía, de este mal!*
> *Quitame, quitame todo el sufrimiento!*
> *Librame librame, madre mía, de todo enemigo!*
> *Librame librame, madre mía!*

✦

> *Liberate me, mother of mine, of all this!*
> *Rip away all of my suffering!*
> *Liberate me, mother of mine, of all of my enemies!*
> *Liberate me, liberate me, mother of mine!*

FRIDAY: THE RECITATION TO
BREAK DOWN LANGUAGE BARRIERS

Say it ten to thirteen times at night.

> *Sinceramente te pido, Santa Muerte, que nos entendamos.*
> *Sinceramente te pido, Santa Muerte, que amigx seamos.*
> *Sinceramente te pido, Santa Muerte, que me agarres las manos.*
> *Y así nos conectamos!*

✦

> *I humbly ask you, Santa Muerte, that we understand each other.*
> *I humbly ask you, Santa Muerte, that we build a friendship.*
> *I humbly ask you, Santa Muerte, to hold my hands.*
> *So we can connect!*

SATURDAY: THE RECITATION TO BE A BETTER HUMAN AND TO BE SOCIALLY CONSCIOUS AND KIND TO OTHERS

Say it ten to thirteen times at night.

> *We are all one! We are all earth! We are all water!*
> *We are all astros! We are all jungle beasts! We are all fine particles*
> *of spirit. We are all people! I sing, I cry, I dance, for all of*
> *those who suffer! I sing, I cry, I dance for the end of all pain and*
> *violence imposed upon this world!*

SUNDAY: THE RECITATION TO LET SANTA MUERTE REST

Say it five times at night before bed.

Aquí descansa mi Santita.
Tras su ayuda, estoy pacificada, sanada, y sin preocupación.
Aquí descanza ya, mi reina de mi corazón.

✦

My Santa Muerte rests here. Through her help, my soul is
peaceful, healed, and without so many things to worry about.
Please go to rest, queen of my heart.

HER/THEIR MAGICAL ATTIRE AND SYMBOLS

Santa Muerte is a shape-shifter. Shape-shifting is the ability of a god, spirit, or person to turn into others, and to express themselves as other selves that I call aspects or avatars. They use this ability to be able to do different magical things, such as to conceal themselves or reveal themselves in spirit forms of different ages, sometimes with animalistic characteristics. Because of this ability, Santa Muerte is associated with different colors and objects. Listed below are the ones I like to use with her/them and the ones I find useful for supporting spells.

- ✦ **MAGICAL STAFF:** Most icons depict this as a scythe (like the one the grim reaper has with a sharpened edge), but I see it as a magical staff, which in codices appears with all of the deities. The deities held this to demonstrate their power.

- ✦ **CRYSTAL BALL:** This represents her/their ability to help you gain powers to see into the future and to practice your spiritual gifts. Santa Muerte can help you make predictions and hone your spiritual gifts, especially during tarot reading.

- **EARTH AS A GLOBE:** This represents how she/they takes care of our Earth and all her/their children and all species. It connects her/them to the guardianship role of our Earth.

- **WINGS:** Many Mesoamerican deities had wings[23] so this is associated with the homeland.

- **HEADDRESS OR CROWN:** Santa Muerte is usually crowned in some way, to show her/their connection to the divine world and to separate her/them from the human realm. Crowns are associated with victory, luck, rites, and protection of the head, an important energy center. The headdress is usually feathered and topped with a jaguar or eagle head, a reference to *chamanismo* and war practices and to Afro-Indigenous roots. (Please note that some headdresses are considered particular and special to certain Native American tribes, so make sure to buy a statue of Santa Muerte that references Mesoamerican deities specifically.)

- **ROPE BELT:** This is an important part of her/their attire that a lot of people miss or don't pay attention to. The magical belt is important as it draws in protection and, in rope form, helps you dominate and stop your enemies so they won't harm you. Santa Muerte wears a rope belt

---

23 Itzpapalotl had butterfly wings, for example, and Quetzalcoatl had an aspect known as the feathered serpent.

to help her/them overpower enemies and to protect the belly button and womb.

◆ **PILE OF SKULLS:** (Not all statues have this.) The Santa Muerte figure stands on mounds of skulls to associate her/them with death realities and the many types of underworld and underground passageways and realities. This also associates Santa Muerte with her/their role as an escort to the realities and as a guide through the passages of death; some are more challenging or frightful, and she/they can guide you to eternal life realities that are more pleasant or through phases in your life analogous to those treks.

◆ **SEQUINS AND GLITTER:** These became common decorations in the Santa Muerte practice when she/they emerged as an important figure among drag queen communities. The sequins are always meant to make her/them look more fabulous and special.

◆ **OWL:** Owls are spirit travelers, meaning they are messengers. Santa Muerte is depicted with an owl sometimes to symbolize wisdom and her/their magical abilities and how she/they communicates between the realities.

◆ **KEYS:** These are symbols of prosperity and of the roads to success being opened.

◆ **HORSESHOE:** Another way that the Santa Muerte image can be depicted is inside of a horseshoe with charged seeds, beans, glitter, and ribbons.

THE CLOAKS AND THEIR COLORS

Below I have listed the different-colored cloaks that Santa Muerte traditionally wears to convey a different facet of her/their personality. Read the following to identify which aspect of Santa Muerte is best for your practice and know when to switch to a certain cloak or add it into your life.

Each of these cloaked versions of her/them responds best to a specific petition. Write the petition on the back of every candle you burn to make contact with that aspect of Santa Muerte and whenever you feel that petition applies to what you need. (Those petitions can also be used as oral worship.) I usually don't use the prayers on the back of the Santa Muerte glass candle because I believe the petitions I have provided here are more effective than traditional religious prayers.

Black Cloak

This Santa Muerte shows no mercy to those who deserve none. She/they punishes criminals and abusers and enacts justice when you are being abused and wronged. She/they is connected to physical strength, decay, dead bodies, cemeteries, and burials. She/they protects those in dangerous professions and those who are in prisons or were formerly imprisoned.

Her/their personality is fierce and dominant, and this is the spookiest[24] of all her/their aspects. I consider her/them the queen of esoteric knowledge. She/they enjoys helping with all spells and teaching you to be better. If you hear a voice telling you to do certain things with candles or other spell tools when you start to practice with her/them, that is Santa Muerte guiding you to make your spells more effective (you can adapt any of these spells and petitions). The voice should sound sweet and be very instructive in giving you spiritual knowledge only, not asking you for anything. She/they can resolve conflict and also is supportive of your living a free path when it comes to hexing mentality.[25]

---

24 Subjectively, to those who are scared easily by gore, blood, and actual death
25 My concept of living a more free way is around the topic of hexing and "dark magic." This is how I can truly live as a bruja, being honest with myself and not ejecting the part of this work that is called hexing completely out of the picture.

Santa Muerte Negra Petition

> Santa Muerte Negra, Madre bondadosa y madre fiera,
> llename de tu fuerza!
> Santa Muerte Negra, ayudame a ser afortunadx, respetadx,
> y ricx!
> Por favor Ayudame a derrumbar y dominar a mis enemigos.
> Cuidame todas las noches en toda oscuridad,
> protegeme de daño, violencia, y odio!

✦

> Black Santa Muerte, kind mother, fierce mother. Fill me with
> your strength! Black Santa Muerte, help me be fortunate,
> respected, and rich. Help me defeat and dominate my enemies.
> Watch over me at night, protect me from harm, violence,
> and hate!

Black Santa Muerte Spray

- ✦ 4 drops ginger essential oil
- ✦ 20 drops cedarwood essential oil
- ✦ 30 drops lemon essential oil
- ✦ 20 drops rosemary essential oil
- ✦ 40 drops chamomile essential oil

Blue Cloak

The blue cloak of Santa Muerte is associated with intellectual endeavors such as learning a new language, memory, attending school, exam success, and professional goals. She/they is also useful for urgent or unexpected matters such as when there is an accident or someone falls ill. She/they can help you help others especially when situations are desperate or hopeless.

She/they can help you calm other people and assist their mental peace. If you want to do healing work on someone, this Santa Muerte helps with distance healing work and doing spell work favors for others. She/they helps with healing after infidelity.

Santa Muerte Azul Petition

Santa Muerte Azul, gracias por tu ayuda inmediata!
Gracias por tu ayuda en situaciones urgentes!
Ayudame, Santa Muerte, limpiame, ayudame a perdonar, a sanar,
y ayudame a mandarle energía a ____. Limpia la energía de ____.
[Insert the name of the people you would like to help and
devote energy to here.]

✦

Blue Santa Muerte, thank you for your fast help!
Thank you for your help in urgent matters!
Help me to forgive, to heal, and help me to cleanse myself and
cleanse ____. Help me to send ____ healing energy today. [Insert the
name of the people you would like to help and devote energy to here.]

Blue Santa Muerte Spray

- 3 ounces witch hazel
- 60 drops cedarwood oil

Brown Cloak

This is the aspect of Santa Muerte connected to fertility and sex, home magic, medicine, children, animals, and foods. This Santa Muerte assists those who perform limpias and energy work. She/they can resolve conflict and help in relationships. She/they helps with getting out of abusive situations. The brown color represents the blending of different energies when it comes to magic and spells, and she/they supports living a free path when it comes to hexing.[26] This aspect of Santa Muerte is very drawn to people who are more withdrawn and quiet, or those who have speech impediments and hearing impediments, as well as to those who feel like outcasts or who struggle to socialize. She/they can help heal loneliness.

Santa Muerte Marrón Petition

Santita, tú que eres mi amiga y mi compañera.
Cuando me siento solo/a/x, consolame,
Cuando me sienta perdida/x/o, levantame!
Liberame de toda cadena y todo cordón de energía que
me quiera destruir o dañar!

---

26 Living as a free witch means being able to cast hexes if you want and when you feel it is justified. This part of the lifestyle is optional, but it allows for you to work with this type of magic without stigmatizing its use before you really get to know it. Most witchcraft authors I have read recommend staying in the area of "white magic" without practicing hexes, but I encourage people to explore, and this is what I have been taught and what has made me successful. I absolutely must stress this does not mean to kill and to cause accidents or illnesses or anything else you wouldn't want to happen to you because hexing is about correcting energy issues, *not* about causing someone damage. This is how you won't suffer from hexing. Hexing without thought and with evil intent only is going to bounce back on you, but when it is more justified, that is okay.

✦

> *Santa Muerte, my friend, my companion.*
> *When I'm alone, console me!*
> *When I'm lost and confused, uplift me!*
> *Unchain and liberate me from all ropes and chains to*
> *energies that may harm or destroy me!*

Santa Muerte Marrón Spray

- 3 ounces witch hazel
- 30 drops amber essential oil

Gold Cloak

This is the Santa Muerte related to luck! She/they helps with all matters of fortune and business. Gold Santa Muerte's personality is mild. She/they is alert, vigilant, and protective, like a war deity. This Santa Muerte has really helped me with my social media presence and praising her/them may make you more successful in terms of sponsorships, ad revenue, and other advertising money.

SANTA MUERTE ALTAR

Her/their altar can be in any room that is not your bedroom unless she/they gives you permission to keep an altar there. She/they may do this if she/they understands you have limited space. Her/their altar should have a statue, and the altar will not be "active" until she/they has a statue, portrait, or other vessel to enter. The statue colors I recommend for beginners are white, black, and gold.

For her/their altar, you will need:

- Incense burner
- 1 glass for water to refresh daily
- 1 special coffee and tea cup so you can share hot beverages with her/them
- 1 champagne flute for when she/they asks for something fancy like tequila or flavored liqueurs or champagne
- 1 Santa Muerte candle, of any color that resonates with you
- Big pieces of crystal quartz
- Little chest with jewels to gift her/them (they don't have to be expensive but things like ornate earrings or sparkly big hoops fascinate her/them and can actually be put on certain statues)
- 1 Santa Muerte *medalla*, or talisman, in gold or gold coated, kept in a red silk cloth for protection
- Her/their favorite offerings, which include apples, oranges, prepared candles, herbal joints, cigars, beers, candy and chocolates, lots of fresh flowers, and freshly prepared foods
- 1 white sheet to cover her/their statue when guests come over or when you feel it is appropriate to block her/them out of respect

After you spend a few months getting to know her/them and really testing the waters, you can then place candles, images, and statues of Santa Muerte on your spell work altar so she/they can help you.

MEDALLA BLESSING RITUAL

The medalla is a beautiful protective pendant that represents Santa Muerte. It is worn to show you are a proud devotee. You don't have to buy an expensive one to please her/them. Many are available that are not made of expensive metals. However, if you are able to afford a gold-coated or real gold medalla, then get one because it will last you longer.

You will need:

- Incense burner
- Charcoal
- Myrrh powder
- Fresh white flowers
- Protection spray
- Receive Messages oil
- Witch hazel
- 3-ounce glass bottle
- 20 drops neroli fragrance oil
- Santa Muerte sprays
- Clean bowl with a generous serving of five freshly washed peaches
- 1 100-peso bill
- 1 small jar of honey

Kneel before the altar of Santa Muerte at midnight on a full moon and let her/them know that you have brought peaches, flowers, and honey for her/them! Place the offerings on the altar. Let her/them enjoy them for about five minutes and then proceed to bring the medalla to her/them. Place it at the feet of her/their statue. Bow before Santa Muerte, and then spray all three sprays on the medalla, over the statue, and over your offerings. Spray from about two or three feet away from the medalla.

WELCOME HER/THEM IN RITUAL

To welcome Santa Muerte into your home and into your spiritual practice, you will need:

- 2 3-by-18-inch white pillar candles
- 1 white skull candle
- 1 3-by-18-inch green candle

- ✦ 1 Santa Muerte statue
- ✦ Santa Muerte oil
- ✦ 1 Santa Muerte medalla
- ✦ 1 wax stick
- ✦ Mint
- ✦ Goldenseal
- ✦ Lady's mantle
- ✦ 1 bottle of red wine or champagne

The white pillar candles should be prepared with only Santa Muerte oil and should not be stuffed with loose herbs. Place the candles on the candle-burning plate in this order: white, green, white. Place them in the shape of a crescent moon with the points facing down, and then stuff the white skull candle with herbs and pour Santa Muerte oil over it as well. This can be made even more special if you wear ritual attire, such as a long white satin ribbon to tie your hair in a braid away from your face if you have long hair. Or wear a plain white shirt and black flowing pants or a flowing skirt to honor her/them as a deity of justice and duality. Put on your Santa Muerte medalla. Light the candles.

Kneel before her/them at the altar and let her/them know you are there. Converse with her/them and share things, be emotional, be real, and trust in her/them. At the end, stand up, hold the bottle in front of the altar, present it proudly, and pour her a drink. Don't drink any yourself, and serve her daily until you run out.

Afterword

T hank you for taking this journey with me! To conclude I just want to share a poem with you, to inspire you, to connect you to your power, and to help you prepare to meet spirit guides. I am so glad you joined me to learn!

Across the skies I form a bridge!
I can reach any ocean, and feel every ground.
My wise old grandma guides me across graveyards
and ghost towns.
My cackling grandpa reveals secret and mysterious things.
I'm instantly lifted, I'm flapping my wings,
messages, messages, may all my guides bring.

Appendix 1:
Crystal Index

AMAZONITE: It brings people with big egos the gift of humility. It is very loving and helps people unite under one cause. This crystal comforts people who are dying and gives the dying a helping hand to get to the other side. It aids those who do death doula work.

AMBER: Amber is not a crystal but hardened matter with great healing capacities. It extends your life and can be used in spells to heal people. Amber is very valuable, so it helps draw in abundance.

AMETHYST: Above all, this is a crystal for love spells. It casts a powerful enchanting energy on your target, and it also promotes spiritual visions and connection, which is why many people call it a third-eye-opening crystal. It helps people who are shy overcome nervousness. Amethyst cleanses jealousy away and replaces it with loving vibes. It is useful for defeating enemies via hexes and reversal, domination, and confusion spells. (Some crystals can help you cast payback spells because crystals aren't going to judge you for doing what is necessary.)

AMETRINE: This is a lovely blended crystal that is half pure amethyst and half heat-treated amethyst. This crystal supports healing journeys, encourages gentleness, and helps dispel negative self-image. It can make you feel beautiful and support appearance changes. Additionally, it supports studying and memory, particularly for those who study law.

ANGEL AURA QUARTZ: This is a quartz crystal that gets treated with high heat in a vacuum and is coated with fine vaporized precious metals, in most cases silver and platinum. The stone then takes on a very glittery exterior with rainbows in the reflection. This is a super powerful crystal. It protects you on all levels, makes you impenetrable to negative energies, brings out your natural power, and makes you charming and conversational. It fixes energy leaks (when something is causing you to lose energy and become tired or to have the same problems over and over).

APATITE: This crystal is excellent for healing the hands. It also protects you from fatigue and energy loss during the day. Additionally, it sends your messages long distances to others and encourages you to be accepting of yourself. The stone can help build friendships in workplaces.

ARAGONITE: The white kind of aragonite cleanses and clears the entire home when charged correctly. (I would place it in a living room, dining room, or entertainment room.) It has a very large and extensive energy field, so it can be placed at the center of any crystal grid, and it will make the energy last longer and spread out more to the entire body. This elegant crystal draws in intellectual, like-minded people with sophisticated taste. It is great for manifesting money, friendships, business, and the attention of high-profile people. It helps reveal the secrets of others and makes people willing to tell the truth! It helps troubled marriages come back together and can be a really beautiful energy tool to use during weddings and any magical wedding-related ancestral ceremonies.

ASTROPHYLLITE: This crystal uncovers deeply buried emotions and gently brings them to the surface for healing, and then helps you dissolve these buried experiences so they don't damage you any longer. It helps you gather your thoughts and look forward to the next day. It can help you with spells to heal your relationship to your mother. You can buy this crystal and offer it to the grandmother and mother deities, as they like it because of its beauty and calmness.

AZURITE: This stone is very connected to the sentient cosmos (outer space) and can help you travel through the different realities in which the deities live. It is used to draw in help from the guides if they have chosen to assist you in spells. It helps call spirit guides, particularly those who like to teach. This stone helps you feel responsible and helps in trade and business. It increases your powers of persuasion and helps with sending energy long distances.

BERYL: This stone brings hope into your life, responds to your personal vibration, and essentially adapts, changes, listens to you, and performs what it needs to in a smart way to heal you.

BLACK ONYX: This is a very hard stone, which is useful for travel since it won't break easily, and promotes humility, hard work, and a steady income. It is great for anyone who works long hour, as it helps the user survive long shifts and also helps with workplace issues.

BLACK TOURMALINE: This stone deep cleanses all of the energy in the body and leaves you feeling less anxious and clogged by unfortunate energy. This stone acts best on its own when used in spells or on altars to maximize its effect. It also can clear the mind of invasive thoughts and of any thoughts planted by an enemy. This is not a very visionary stone, so it's best used for spells and physical healing. It helps those who have trouble following commands from spirit guides and those who are stubborn and resistant to change or guidance. This stone is super helpful if you are a tarot reader who reads in a public space or shop that isn't your own. It can keep away jealousy, gossip, and fatigue from your reading and protect you from unwanted spirits.

BLUE HOWLITE: It is comforting especially when you are missing home, and it can be used to connect to bird spirit guides. It makes you more ethical and helps you identify and remember your mission in life.

BLUE LACE AGATE: This is a stone that tends to work wonderfully on people who are skeptical about crystals. It is helpful for emotional healing work and for connecting you to those who care about you truly. Use it to draw in ideal friendships. It removes any energies that feel heavy during the day. You can talk to this stone more than others, and it will provide a healing sensation and the feeling that you are heard.

BLUE QUARTZ: This stone slows down the hyperactive mind, makes you peaceful, and prepares you for meditation. It helps you charge other stones by letting you know exactly word by word what you should ask them to do. Rub it on your palms before you hold another crystal to help you with programming others. Use it when you are in the process of letting go of someone or when you miss someone and want to stop thinking of them.

BLUE TIGER'S EYE: This is an excellent shielding stone, as it protects you from psychic attack while at the same time tuning you into a relaxed and uplifting vibration. It has a very strong masculine energy. This stone helps you build for your future and makes you organized and good at planning. This stone works on the solar plexus and takes up all different types of energies in the room and directs them at you for use.

BLUE TOURMALINE: This stone can help you learn a new language or develop new skills. It helps with studying sessions, memorization, test-taking abilities, and easing anxiety.

BRAZILIAN TOPAZ: This stone will help you attract all your desires. It has a magnificent ability to make things happen and to bring in energies from the universe to help you. It works fast and listens to what you ask for, so be careful what you wish for! This crystal will give you a sense that you are on top of the world and may make you feel like a master of the universe, able to pick up spiritual and real-life skills easily. I believe it works on the brain and nervous system to create this powerful energy.

BRECCIATED JASPER: This stone removes scary experiences from the memory and helps you put up a fight and stand your ground when you are being threatened. It functions as a "spirit army" that helps make you more aware of threats and danger and shield yourself.

BROWN TIGER'S EYE: This is an excellent stone to help heal physical ailments related to the digestive system. This helps with the body's circulatory processes and supports fitness goals and muscle growth. Place it on bone injuries to heal them faster.

BUMBLEBEE JASPER: This stone helps you come up with original and new ideas, externalizes your power so that others can see it, and connects you to outer space guides.

CARIBBEAN CALCITE: This stone is excellent for adding cheer and brightness to a space. It heals the head and shoulders and sexual organs, helps you remember your roots, connects you to your ancestors, and adds a sweet element to spells to draw in love and opportunities. It also supports job and money spells.

CHAROITE: This brilliant crystal is protective of your third eye, as it guards your spirit and your spiritual energy so that nobody can steal it from you. It supports healers who draw in pity cases. It supports long astral travel journeys and can transport you into space during astral travel. Additionally, charoite expands all the senses and makes life more pleasurable. It clears messy and anxious thinking.

CHRYSOCOLLA: This stone can help you make life more exciting. Use it in spells when your life feels stagnant and needs variety. The stone also helps you bring in positive change, especially when it comes to money and new love.

CHRYSOPRASE: This crystal is a great aid to those in the medical profession because it allows you to channel your healing powers and save lives. It supports you in times of high stress and helps you make intuitive decisions. Chrysoprase gives you mental clarity and makes meditation easier when your brain feels crowded.

CINNABRITE: This is a great crystal to help you work through romantic issues when deciding what you want in your ideal partner. It helps you tap into the vibration of your soul mate and attract that person. It works on the head and third-eye chakras.

CITRINE: This stone is an ally to those who are making monetary investments, helping to increase wealth, but it doesn't conjure luck and wealth out of nowhere. It works with existing wealth to multiply it. Citrine also cleanses the aura, removing bad energies and replacing bad thoughts with wholesome ones. This stone helps you reprogram your thoughts. Useful in spells to find homes, to be motivated and career driven, to expand business, and to accomplish large money goals. It works with the crown chakra.

CLEAR QUARTZ: This is the master healer, as it can work on any health issue and cleanse difficult energies. Clear quartz is excellent for ending the day, to release all negativity and to harmonize all of the chakras before bedtime. Clear quartz is excellent for building healing routines and for increasing and clearing communication to the spirit world. It is an excellent crystal to use with water, especially in baths and teas.

CRAZY LACE AGATE: This stone makes you forget your troubles and allows you to tap into an energy plane that is removed from worry. It promotes clean sexual energy, helps you avoid gossipers, and helps you listen to your true self. Use it in a *tapa boca* spell, in an ancestral communication spell, or in a spell to draw in multiple lovers.

DALMATIAN JASPER: This crystal helps people get along and helps you be a firm parent. It also fixes issues in the home. It works on the root and solar plexus chakras.

DENDRITIC AGATE: This crystal supports you during seasonal depression and allows you to internalize lessons you are having trouble grasping. This stone supports the penis and is connected to the nervous system, the circulatory system, and the small blood vessels of the body. It has the miraculous ability to detox the body and help maintain nice skin. It works on the heart chakra and the root chakra.

EMERALD: This crystal is useful for any type of visionary quest. Emerald makes you confident and bold. Thus it is a great ally for public speakers and performers. Emerald helps you pick all the right words to communicate, and it has an effect on how you receive and choose the words you speak. Emerald can magnify the effects of your spells, so it is good to always have on the altar when casting.

FLUORITE: It is a master crystal for gaining spiritual insight and clear visions. This is also a master healer. Green fluorite is excellent for supporting tarot readings, helping you focus and increasing the number of predictions you can make per reading. Green fluorite is a great massage stone as it promotes the healing of the physical and spiritual bodies. Purple or pink fluorite helps increase empathy. Fluorite helps you spiritually connect to your clients and listen to their pain but not absorb it. It can be used by a brujx to help draw out bad energies and make them more visible so they are easier to target. Use it universally in spells, as it can lend itself to almost anything!

GARNET: This stone helps with menstrual cycle irregularities and menstrual complaints. It seals up the body so nothing comes in when you truly need to be private. It is useful when you are under spiritual attack. Garnet helps you ace tests. It is a great stone to hold on to while you cry to ground you during emotional episodes. Use garnet in a wearable talisman. Garnet in limestone helps you have a green thumb. It supports plant growth and soil health and allows you to understand and speak to plant spirits better. It's a good gardening ally.

GOLDEN LABRADORITE: This stone radiates a lot of energy. Thus in a grid it increases and reaches all other stones, forming an energetic connection to all of them and helping them work together. This stone is a gentle healer that soothes the body, mind, and soul.

GREEN AVENTURINE: This crystal supports the sick and lends healing energy to pull you through illness. It also purifies thoughts and envelops the body in a protective veil to keep away injustices, wrongdoings, and bad luck. Use it in uncrossing and unhexing spells.

GREEN ONYX: This stone supports all health goals, strengthens your bonds to others, and builds strong families. It is connected to the heart chakra and the solar plexus chakra and corresponds to the sun and Mother Earth.

GROSSULARITE GARNET/GREEN GARNET: This stone helps you pay attention and be calm. This is a very good stone for people with panic issues or those suffering from PTSD. It can be very caring, if asked. Garnet is the stone of romantics and lovers. It helps you reach relationship milestones such as engagement and marriage. Garnet also supports infants and assures them a rich future. It is great as a gift for new parents and for welcoming a baby to a new home.

HEMATITE: This is one of the most powerful protection stones. It helps you consciously deflect bad energy, so it is best used as jewelry in conjunction with your mental powers to shoo away bad energies or to enact immediate protection when something has bothered your energy. Hematite helps you build stronger relationships and career foundations.

HEMATOID QUARTZ: This stone helps you stop pretending to be someone else and supports you during identity changes. It heals insecurities and helps you move on fast after heartbreak. Hematoid quartz connects with the heart and crown chakras.

HOWLITE: This stone is used for personal strength, energy field strengthening, and magnetism. Howlite, especially white howlite, draws in beautiful angelic energies, opens the third eye, and enhances lucid dreaming. Use it in spells to support psychic visions. White howlite is also supportive of artists and creative minds, helping you overcome criticism and self-doubt. It corresponds with the heart and the crown chakras. It works to heal the head, especially the lips, neck, and upper chest. White howlite also keeps away bad spirits. Blue howlite is a comforting stone, especially when you are missing home. It can be used to connect to bird spirit guides. It is also a stone that helps you be more ethical and identify and remember your mission in life.

IOLITE: This stone is for those who already have an open third eye. This will help you get to new levels of abilities and visions. Iolite corresponds with the solar plexus chakra. You can use this crystal to practice dominance and obsession magic, placing the thoughts you want someone to have about you.

K2 CRYSTAL: This crystal supports the crown chakra. It makes you present and attentive, promotes wakefulness, and gives you extra strength to go through the day. It helps get you up in the morning and helps with morning routines and maintaining structure.

KAMBABA JASPER: This crystal helps you build strong walls of energy protection. It is excellent for communicating with the spirit reality and it has a sophisticated and put-together energy that is excellent anytime you feel unprofessional or nervous in a job setting. It helps you adjust. It can be used to summon money. It can also be used when you need to be respected as a figure of authority as it will help others see you as more respectful.

KUNZITE: This stone promotes peace, tranquility, fluidity, and free-spiritedness. It helps you hear your intuition and discover your soul's gifts. Kunzite bonds intensely with musicians. This crystal is very useful for helping you shield yourself from negative energy. It has such a divine high vibration and a penetrating calm energy.

LABRADORITE: This crystal supports deep meditation and helps connect you to memories of your past life. It makes you captivating and interesting. Labradorite heals the throat and third-eye chakras, and the eyes. Labradorite tells you about the next day. When the sun rises, pull up your labradorite, make some tea, meditate, and ask the stone to help you know what's to come.

LAPIS LAZULI: This stone works on all the chakras and supports you during surgery. It also supports organ health.

LARIMAR: This stone assists in the study of nature and yerberia studies, and it is a great stone for helping you see water spirits and connect to water. This herb also assists in generational healing. It can help you connect to your soul mate, as well as help strengthen a marriage.

LARVIKITE: This stone helps you connect to nighttime spirits and find them in their hiding places during meditation. It also makes you feel intelligent and bold and amplifies masculine energy. It helps build layers to your personality to make you more interesting and fresh. For male-identified persons, it helps you pick up women, supports sexual vigor, and draws in handsome partners. It draws out toxins from your immediate environment, making each space and place cleansed before you enter. You can use it to purify spaces before you enter them. It also helps you distance yourself from work and supports your ability to make accurate predictions.

LEOPARD SKIN JASPER: This stone supports fitness goals, especially the growth of the muscles. It promotes long, restful sleep and is connected to the sky and to the Earth. It corresponds with the nasal passages and the third-eye and throat chakras. It is of course connected to jungle cats.

LEPIDOLITE: This stone helps you be the star in meetings and formal workplaces. It helps you feel gorgeous and rich. This stone is perfect for those looking to manifest luxury. Don't put this stone in water to clean—instead use a polishing cloth to keep it shiny.

MALACHITE: This is a good-luck stone. This stone is connected to the animal realm, particularly reptiles, amphibians, and big cats. Use it to work with these energies in spirit and to contact them for your work. Malachite helps the lungs and expels phlegm, so use it for alkaline breath work. This stone corresponds to the crown and third-eye chakras. It is particularly influential for the ears as well as the neck and shoulders. Malachite jewelry helps you become a healer and evoke healing energy in the world effortlessly. It also helps spark motivation.

MONTANA AGATE: This stone helps you overcome intergenerational differences and come closer to your elders. It is a time stone, meaning that it can be used to remember the past and the ties between past, present, and future. It's a great stone to put on your tarot deck.

MOOKAITE: This is a type of yellow-and-burgundy jasper that is excellent for promoting restfulness and calm. It also promotes patience and slows things down. Mookaite has a very supportive and mothering energy and is an excellent healing crystal for new mothers or struggling mothers. Mookaite prevents nausea, helps the body absorb nutrients, and assists those who suffer from suicidal ideation. It reminds you to get up every morning and gives you energy to make it through the day. Mookaite works on the heart and crown chakras.

OBSIDIAN BALL: This stone is the ultimate source of knowledge, containing the entire universe. It is a perfect healing companion with feminine nurturing energy that works great to comfort the soul.

OCEAN JASPER: This stone can send out punishments and cause bitterness and overwhelming sadness if you wish to cause that to someone else. Conversely, the stone can remove those same vibrations from an aura. Work with it on your crown chakra via the scalp. Rub it around the entire perimeter of your face in a circle to relieve yourself from the fatigue of the day. It helps you conjure jewels.

OPALITE: This is a synthetic magical "stone." The stone is good for outdoor spells because it brings in the sunlight in a very lively and special way. Use it to harness sunlight on particularly cheery days. Empowered with the sun, it can help plants grow, help you feel uplifted, and magnify the power of other stones. It will also work well if you put it in water to charge the water for spells. Opalite pairs excellently with rose quartz, turquoise, larimar, dark amethyst, and ruby.

ORANGE CALCITE: This stone is full of light and beams out into rooms. It is a space-clearing crystal, meant to be used in larger pieces to add good, fortunate energy. Excellent for daily meditation! It works best with the whole body and when held at the navel during meditation with both hands. Use it to bring love into the whole world!

PEACH MOONSTONE: This stone supports those who want to become more quiet and still, heals headaches, and can heal skin ailments. It clears the third eye and connects you to the sacred geometry realm.

PERIDOT: This stone makes everybody like you, turning your haters into friends. The body can really absorb the powers of this stone. Use it to charge your hands before ritual work or healing work.

PINK CALCITE: This stone helps you connect to your true voice. Very few crystals work to heal the physical eye, but pink calcite is one of them. It also soothes and removes impurities from the throat.

PINK OPAL: This crystal can heal issues of the mouth and tongue, support the healing of soft tissue injuries, and help keep you young. It helps the ears and may help you have out-of-body experiences.

PISTACHIO CALCITE: This stone helps you make mature financial decisions, makes others around you more pleasant, and brings out kindness. It is a great ally for those dealing with mood disorders that involve anger. This stone connects you to the heart chakra.

PREHNITE: This stone wakes up abilities that are latent, unlocks talents, and increases your understanding of esoteric knowledge. It is connected to the heart and third-eye chakras.

PYRITE: This stone is an excellent protection crystal. Use it in all protection spells. The crystal is also feisty in the sense that it can lend strength to a spell meant to return energy to the sender or a love spell on someone you want to marry.

RED CORAL: This stone is particularly useful for medicine work as it heals the limbs and sexual organs.

RED TIGER'S EYE: This stone has a strong feminine warrior energy to support people through emotional times. It gives the person strength mentally and helps facilitate sleep during grieving. It also helps relieve desperation. Red tiger's eye assists in grief support spells, limpias, and with any menstrual cycle or womb magic.

RHODONITE: This stone heals the wounds that have been caused by heartbreak, disappointment, and loss of loved ones. It supports you in times of grief.

ROOT BEER CALCITE: This crystal helps you be responsible. It is a great ally for working people trying to move up the ladder. Due to its café con leche color, it gives you an energy boost and makes you alert. It brings out your inner elder and your inner sage.

ROSE QUARTZ: This stone fills the body with a feeling of love, stopping self-hatred and encouraging you to see yourself positively. It assists in emotional healing and has a warm, protective energy that gets cast on the user like a shield. It pairs well with howlite, selenite, and spirit quartz. Rose quartz corresponds to the arms, the fingers and toes, and the crown and root chakras.

RUBY: This stone brings out your best qualities. It supports spiritual growth and development, heals all the chakras, and repairs energy leaks and energy problems. It is an awesome crystal to support you through sickness. It is good for performing magic for your beloveds, to cast spells for them so they also triumph. Ruby assists in money magic and is great in charm bags for money. All rubies replenish and refine energy during the day, working on the mechanisms of the chakras. They help keep good energy flowing through all the chakras.

RUBY IN FELDSPAR: This crystal is very calming and allows you to take it easy. It helps you bring in money and feel creative. It supports those who have a more shy sexual personality. Working with the crystal can make you more adventurous. It also heals sexual discomfort and reproductive health issues. It is associated with the root and solar plexus chakras.

RUBY IN FUCHSITE: This is a really positive crystal that catches your negative thoughts and turns them into positive ones. It can be used to direct love and healing energy to the wounds of love or abandonment, heal attachments, and help you make changes. It works on the third-eye, heart, and root chakras. It helps your children become more independent and can be used to communicate better with them.

RUBY IN ZOISITE: This crystal supports happiness and gives you creative ideas. Ruby in zoisite also helps you divine questions about love and your perfect soul mates. This ruby heals the heart chakra. It also strengthens the hands, meaning that it is a great crystal for those who work a lot with their hands.

SARDONYX: This crystal absorbs energy, so you can use it to bring any energy you want more of into your life. It essentially manifests the effects of whatever it's around. For example, if you want it to absorb the vibration of a particular country, you would take it there with you! Sardonyx holds memories and helps you recall a past life. It is a teaching stone, so use it when you have students.

SCOLECITE: This is a very purifying stone that helps you reach "insane" goals, so this is one to use when you are really shooting for the stars in spells and manifestations. It pairs particularly well with gold to attract superior spirit guides, those of gods and legendary figures.

SELENITE: This stone pulls you out of difficult situations, helps you during crisis, helps you petition for stable income, protects you from harmful entities, protects your space, and connects you to your spirit guides. It is connected to the third-eye and sacral chakras. It heals the body, especially the feet and toes, and activates and amplifies the energy of other crystals.

SHIVA LINGAM: This stone guards your possessions and your altar while you are away. The combination of these energies grounds you during meditation. It supports sexual healing and healing from abuse.

SMOKY QUARTZ: This is a gazing stone that penetrates your eyes to heal the brain and nervous system. It relieves tension, anxiety, and stress, and helps heal addictions. This stone absorbs bad vibrations, so cleanse it often and keep it shiny for best results.

SODALITE: The white in this stone is protective and cleansing. It also stimulates spiritual visions. The dark blue has a capacity to call your energies inward and to prepare for meditation. It assists in cleansing spells and spells for vision development.

STRAWBERRY QUARTZ: This stone extends your aura's energy, relieves fear, aids in meditation, makes you girly in personality, behavior, and appearance, and makes you patient with others. It is the perfect crystal for self-improvement journeys. It pairs well with pyrite, mookaite, and gold sheen obsidian. It corresponds with the spine, the ears, the heart, the belly and belly button, and the skin of the face. It is an ally to breast cancer survivors or breast cancer patients.

SUNSTONE: This is a great stone to work with in the summertime as its powers are maximized then. It promotes flexibility and healthy exercise habits and is a great ally to athletes and competitors. It increases business. It can make your magic petitions happen rapidly.

TOURMALATED QUARTZ: This lovely crystal is protective and cleanses spaces. It is a good crystal for supporting protection spells and erasing bad energy experiences. Use it to support yourself after difficult days.

TURQUOISE: This stone harmonizes energy and brings great energy into all of your centers. Turquoise is a valuable stone that helps you conjure money. Turquoise helps with sexual and reproductive health and increases life's pleasures. Turquoise heals the heart after heartbreak and makes it stronger.

UNAKITE: This stone is a flat energy stone that can be used when someone needs an energy to be tamed within them. It heals the heart by detoxing it of bad vibrations. Protect your heart with unakite when dating. It helps sensitive and empathic people carry energy without severe damage. Aids the liver and tongue and vagina and anus.

WHITE MOONSTONE: Usually this moonstone has rainbows within the white structure and black markings as well. It is an excellent stone for supporting all spells, connecting you to the cycles of the moon, and promoting love, infatuation, and romance.

WHITE OPAL: This stone is great for attracting perfect love and perfect marriage. It aids married couples in fixing issues. It is great when used on the body to calm energy, especially for winding down at night. It promotes a healthy night's sleep and helps you wake refreshed and clear, fixing issues of the skin.

YELLOW OPAL: I find that this crystal helps you communicate with any astral energies, including those of extraterrestrial beings, but also the stars and celestial objects themselves. It encourages your ability to see things in other realities and far up into the sky and space. It makes you smooth and easy to talk to so it can aid in dating and helping you fight insecurities.

ZEBRA JASPER: This is a phenomenal crystal for attracting wealth and money. Jasper has an alluring quality, so it helps with attraction of high-quality sophisticated people into your life. It aids in sales and business. This crystal is capable of cleansing the energy of an entire space, bringing it beauty and stabilizing it. This stone supports customer service skills and prevents energy drains while at work.

Appendix 2:
Yerbas of Brujeria

Agrimony: This herb causes bitterness, so it is good for vengeful spells. It has an amazing ability to keep away thieves and help people get out of jail. It keeps people from telling lies about you on the stand.

Arnica: It is a very strong protection herb. This herb can be used to connect to midwife spirits. The herb is great for the skin and for healing wounds, and it helps with spells to conquer enemies. Don't ingest it.

Avocado Leaf: This is a plant you use when you need help in emergencies! It's great for when an unexpected tragedy occurs. It helps you deal with money problems such as bankruptcy. Generally it is very protective and makes it hard for your enemies to spy on you or be able to get to you. It can help you hide a deep secret. It can be burned to summon Earth deities. It gives you spiritual and physical strength and protects you from the law and from spiritual attack. It is also really useful in writing petitions. Write on the leaf to send your petition to the spirit world.

Bearberry (Uva Ursi): This is an herb that helps conjure love. It is useful for keeping lovers faithful and for bringing a relationship out of a rut.

Bee Pollen: Although it isn't a plant, I include it here because of its capability to cast powerful magic. It can conjure luck. It is used in love spells.

BLADDER WRACK: Use it to send negative energies back to your enemies. It is useful for protecting against astral attacks. It can cause depression in a person. It can drain and take away energy from enemies. It helps those who have a lot of burdens to bear, including busy mothers.

BLESSED THISTLE: This is my ultimate favorite money herb. It is excellent for attracting marriage, protecting the family, and calling in money. It is also good for calling in adventure and spontaneity. Use it to protect your valuables.

BONESET: This herb gets rid of terrible and scary energies. It is used to shield yourself from jealousy and bad people. It helps you enforce your personal space.

BUTCHER'S BROOM: This protects the home and your possessions. It protects against demonic attacks. It helps people with marital problems and helps draw in a marriage proposal.

CALAMUS ROOT: It helps those who get embarrassed easily. It helps with eloquence and public speaking. It helps to draw in jobs. This herb is useful in all spells to get justice and to win over an enemy.

CALENDULA: Use it for spells of happiness, healing, and magic to honor the dead. It is also an herb of beauty, so it can be used in health spells to heal the skin and organs.

CATNIP: This is a plant that helps remove gossip and slander. It is useful when you have enemies who are actively trying to ruin you. Use this to confuse them. Catnip is a duality herb, meaning it can conjure love but also cause breakups, and it can be used to send spiritual attacks to others. Catnip is an herb of the moon.

CENTAURY: This plant helps heal sibling relationships. It is an herb to attract travel opportunities. It increases the sense of adventure in life and promotes longevity.

CHAMOMILE: This plant promotes sleep. It is used to conjure money and to bless marriages and help couples who are on the brink of divorce. Use it to protect from eclipses and retrograde planets.

CHAPARRAL: This is protective during times of war. It prevents attack by dogs and wild animals. This herb is useful for protection during travel. It is an herb of Sagittarius. It really helps those who want to be in a leadership or respected teaching role. It helps lawyers win in court.

CORN SILK: This herb is used to make contact with human spirits. It makes a great substitute for hair when asked for in a spell. It is powerful in drawing in multiple lovers, making it a great ally to those who are single. You can use it to freeze and stop your enemies from harming you. It can cause harm if that is something you justify. It calls on the spirits of elders.

DAMIANA: This is an herb to conjure love and lust. This herb connects you to sacred sexuality and makes you more psychic. Damiana helps improve the appearance and aids in beauty spells.

DANDELION LEAF: This herb works on the emotions to soothe them. It helps heal heartbreak. It can conceal you from your enemies. It is excellent for spirit communication spells and spells to reveal the future.

DANDELION ROOT: This plant holds a lot of solar energy, so it is very effective in cleansing and empowering the body and for doing fertility and protection spells.

DEVIL'S CLAW ROOT: This is a very protective root. It helps with lineage healing and clearing ancestral energies. Devil's claw is powerful for cleansing spells. It helps in spells to dominate men. This herb clears energies buried deep inside you and clears subconscious memories.

ELDERFLOWER: It makes you feel beautiful and helps you do glamour spells where you write down how you want to look. It is excellent for healing the skin and nails. It is great for use in tea leaf readings. It improves spiritual sight and helps you clarify your visions. It can be used in spells to channel resurrection energy.

EPAZOTE: This is a really strong and defensive herb. It helps you remove blockages. This is a particularly good herb for healing those who have been in the military or have been affected by war crimes. It gives you insight into your roots.

EUCALYPTUS: This herb helps you make accurate predictions. It is great for opening up the nasal passageways and sweeping away bad energies. It is great for cleansing the home. It is used in spells to repel the law or free prisoners.

FIG LEAF: This is a luck herb. It can be used to send spirits back to where they came from and draw boundaries with them. It stimulates creativity. It helps with digestion spells. It brings riches.

GALANGAL: It has the capacity to increase the strength of other herbs. Galangal helps with the muscular system. This root assists in healing from abuse and letting the survivor of abuse rise above the situation. It is an herb that encourages loyalty so it can be used to build clientele and customers. It aids in business spells.

GINGKO: It helps you through financial challenges and supports those who perform in the arts.

GOLDENSEAL: This herb increases privacy and makes your neighborhood safer. It is an herb that protects against negative spirits and keeps them from doing harm. The herb removes bad luck. Goldenseal heals all ailments and can be used universally in healing spells. It helps you connect to healing spirit guides.

GREEN TEA LEAF: This improves musical abilities and can help in pregnancy spells. Green tea is great for conjuring wisdom, communicating with spirit guides, and summoning them in spells. It helps you in astral travel.

HIBISCUS: It is great in breakup spells, specifically when used to make someone bitter. It can help you send bitterness and gossip back to the sender. It can break hexes. It can be used to connect to the menstrual cycle, the moon, and to heal the cervix, uterus, fallopian tubes, and ovaries.

HOPS FLOWER: It promotes romance and is great for home protection and home cleansing. It makes people more lively, so it is good to use when you are planning an event that needs to be energetic. It heals grief. It is an herb that helps you predict the future. It makes you see life in a more romantic and hopeful way.

HOREHOUND: It removes hexes. It is a plant that can help you feel fulfilled and successful. It helps connect you to spirit guides. It helps you heal through grief.

HYSSOP: This is an herb that promotes optimism, spiritual connection, riches, and wealth. This is an herb that helps you have a fresh start. It cleanses the mind.

JASMINE FLOWER: It blesses unions and marriages. It is used for justice and is great for those who work in social justice to use in asking for victories. Jasmine is excellent at bringing out sweet personality traits. It helps improve spiritual abilities. It is very powerful for conjuring money.

LADY'S MANTLE: This herb helps protect a childbearing parent and their children. The herb gives you warrior strength. It is an herb that makes travel smoother. It helps you with forgiveness and supports compassion toward yourself.

LAVENDER: This is an herb that promotes relaxation, sleep, and peace. Lavender is useful in love spells. It can help you move into new phases of life.

LEMONGRASS: I use this herb in healing spells and uncrossing spells and to reduce anxiety and ease stomach problems. It is an herb that helps smooth communication and aids in conflict resolution. It is great in helping you avoid the law and win in court. It can be used to give spells long-lasting effects.

LEMON VERBENA: This herb helps you perform in the workplace. It also increases libido and romance. It can be used in beauty spells to improve the appearance. The herb relieves gas problems and helps upset stomachs or nerves.

LICORICE ROOT: It helps you keep a positive mindset. This is great in powder or root form. It is great mixed in incense. Spirits are drawn to it, so use it to summon guides.

LINDEN FLOWER AND LEAF: They are incredibly calming, and they heal ear problems. They help you keep away negative thoughts and nightmares. Linden flower and leaf are useful if you are doing healing spells for a child. They help you heal from grief, abuse, and trauma.

LUNGWORT: It is an herb that conjures wisdom and helps in spells to awaken the third-eye visionary abilities. It helps you make magical contracts (when two or more witches agree to protect one another, for example).

MILK THISTLE SEED: It attracts money. It protects single mothers and children. This herb also prevents energy drains and supports empaths so they don't feel drained. Use it to conjure wisdom.

MOTHERWORT: This is an herb of the sun, and it is androgynous, despite its name. It is great for marriage spells and spells for avoiding divorce. This herb can reveal to you and heal love wounds. This helps you during karmic relationships and can help you avoid making the same mistakes in love. It is an herb that helps prevent bad things from happening, so you can use it if you are really prone to bad luck and need to consistently avoid it.

MULLEIN: It's an herb that works to remove really difficult hexes and crossed conditions. It heals the skin and skeleton. It is great in surgery support spells.

MUSTARD SEED: This seed awakens our past memories. It is connected to the moon. It helps with pregnancy and postpartum healing spells.

MYRRH: It helps cool you down after a heated argument.

MYRTLE: It increases romance and compassion in relationships. It can be used to end arguments and to reach compromises in partnerships. It is a great ally to those who are shy, to give them more courage and drive to shine and be noticed. Myrtle reveals what is called the feminine wisdom of periods and cycles and women's secret powers of domination and sexuality.

OLIVE LEAF: This healing herb is great in limpias. The herb protects you from spirit attack. Olive works universally with goddesses. The olive leaf can also make you victorious and lucky in sports and competitions. The olive leaf helps attract handsome men.

PATCHOULI: This herb covers up your mistakes. It can reconcile you with past lovers and draw in soul mates.

PEONY ROOT: This root helps you rise in your career. It is useful for those who want to create jobs for others and for those who have ideas for a big business.

PERIWINKLE: This herb causes confusion and infatuation. It is also a nighttime herb so you can use it to see better at night and to work with spirits who only come out in nighttime or are associated with dark nights. It helps heal respiratory problems. It prolongs life when someone is close to death; you can try to keep them alive longer using periwinkle in a spell.

PLANTAIN LEAF: It's excellent to use in "pay me back" spells, to collect your debts. Plantain leaf clears energies that are difficult for you to give up on. It helps you through grief and missing recently passed loved ones. It is an herb that helps with skin and bone problems. The herb promotes academic success, and it helps first-generation college students.

RASPBERRY LEAF: It is useful for when you need to come out of a winter rut. It is a very grounding plant, and it helps those who have quick minds to slow down. It can help you with pregnancy spells. This herb is very strong, meaning it can help you set boundaries and protect your energy.

ROWAN TREE BARK: This is a very powerful witchcraft herb. It can be used in spells for protection and for calling on the family line for protection. It is useful for relationship spells, particularly when you want things to move a little slower so you have time to develop true feelings for the person. It can promote honesty, and you can use it on someone to influence them to tell the truth. It helps bring in large sums of money.

SKULLCAP: It is an herb that helps with ancestral connections and helps heal and soothe anxiety, stress, and pain. It can be used to fix karma. It can be used to give someone bad thoughts and to make them hexed.

SLIPPERY ELM: This plant helps you develop fearlessness. The plant is very good at helping you deal with enemies and preventing gossip and slander. You can use it in spells that involve protection from the law and to win court cases. Additionally, it is a sexual herb that can increase libido, pleasure, and sexual activity.

SPEARMINT: This herb makes life easier and can be used to reduce any burden. Spearmint sends healing energy to the realm of the dead, to your ancestors. It purifies spaces. This herb keeps you up at night, so it is good for those who work long shifts or nighttime shifts, as it makes you alert. It is great for fitness goals. It helps grow hair as well and is useful in sexual cleansing spells. It clears bedrooms of bad energy.

STAR ANISE: This herb strengthens most spells and has universal uses. It brings life more dynamic and spontaneous energy.

STEVIA LEAF: It keeps lovers faithful and helps you state what you want in relationships. It can help you attract friends and make career gains.

ST. JOHN'S WORT: This herb heals the sick. It clears the senses when you feel overloaded or clouded. It keeps you in good graces with your spirit guides. It helps with hair growth.

VALERIAN: It is a necromancy herb and helps you live a long life. It soothes the soul and body and also works to relieve anxiety.

VANILLA BEAN: This is excellent for healing depression symptoms and sexual issues and for connecting to the magic of menstrual cycles. This ingredient is excellent for the penis and testicles. It is a very lucky ingredient!

WHEAT: This is a magical ingredient that helps connect you to your ancestors and transport you back in time. Use it to help you astral travel to older times if you feel called to do so. It is capable of sending you back thousands of years. It helps with abundance and is great for conjuring money and improving businesses. It also helps you get up earlier and improves your mornings. Wheat is useful in love spells.

WHITE WILLOW BARK: This is a very calming bark. It tends to cause people to stop arguing and to stop bothering you. It is a third-eye-opening herb, powerful for summoning healing spirits. It helps you *win!*

WILD YAM ROOT: This herb heals hunger and is a great herb for unity. It can help you with healing your ancestors.

WITCH HAZEL: This is what I call a universal use herb. It will do anything for you! It is particularly useful for sending back evil spells and banishing negativity. It can fight off evil entities. It helps in spells to open the third eye.

WOOD BETONY: It helps with abandonment issues in people, including those who have been neglected by parents or caretakers. It helps make parents better. It protects against the loss of a loved one. It aids in gambling. It is a wealth herb.

WOODRUFF LEAVES: This is a feel-good herb, useful for uplifting your mood and having fun and safe astral journeys. It is an herb that helps you attract romantic love, and have success and hot sex in your marriage. It is helpful in making more money.

YARROW: This herb helps in protection magic. It is particularly protective of babies.

YERBA SANTA: It has many uses, even some I'm still discovering, but the primary uses are in healing and health magic. Yerba santa helps improve self-image and helps you connect to your spiritual abilities. It helps with divination and with connecting you to your ancestors. It is an artistic support herb. It can help you conjure money and is a very good herb for those who consider money sacred.

YUCCA ROOT: This is a stamina herb and is great for adding masculine strength to a spell. Yucca helps heal issues with language differences so you can hear your ancestors and learn their languages. This root is also useful for money spells and works well in health spells.

INDEX

ABOUT THE AUTHOR

Valeria Ruelas, "The Mexican Witch," is a gay Chicana/Indigenous bruja/brujx. She/they is a renowned witchcraft author, celebrity tarot reader, expert spell caster, psychic medium, curandera, artist, and spiritual teacher. *Cosmopolitan* has also named her/them one of the most influential witches in the world, and she/they is a regular writer for their witchcraft content. She/they devotes her/their life to studying the occult, astrology, tarot, and Afro-Indigenous magic and producing amazing witchcraft tools and products. She/they is an Aquarius sun, Cancer moon, and Sagittarius rising. She/they is also the owner of a witchcraft store and is currently working on illustrating various tarot decks.